P9-CQM-804

RA Types

Understanding Resident Assistants by Using
the Myers-Briggs Type Indicator® Preferences

Jon K. Coleman
University of Georgia

Published by
Association of College and University Housing Officers-International

Copyright 2003
ISBN 0-945109-08-03

Table of Contents

About the Author iii

Acknowledgements iv

Preface v

Chapter 1 – History and Development of Type Theory 1

Chapter 2 – Preferences and Pairs 5
    Extroversion and Introversion 6
    Sensing and Intuition 8
    Thinking and Feeling 9
    Judging and Perceiving 9

Chapter 3 – Using This Information 13

Chapter 4 – RA Type Descriptions 17
    ISTJ 18
    ISTP 22
    ESTP 26
    ESTJ 30
    ISFJ 34
    ISFP 38
    ESFP 42
    ESFJ 46
    INFJ 50
    INFP 54
    ENFP 58
    ENFJ 63
    INTJ 67
    INTP 72
    ENTP 77
    ENTJ 82

Chapter 5 – Exercises and Applications 87

Chapter 6 – Closing Thoughts 93

Appendix – Suggested Readings and Additional Resources 95

About the Author

Jon Coleman has been working with residence hall leaders and staff since 1988 as a student at the University of Florida. Jon received his B.A. in Political Science and his law degree from the University of Florida, and his M.S.Ed in College Student Personnel at Southern Illinois University in Carbondale. He has been involved with training RA staff and residence-hall student leaders for many years. As an Area Director at Georgia Southern University and Assistant Director of Staff and Student Development at the University of Southern Mississippi, Jon has presented numerous programs on training and leadership. Jon is currently an independent staff trainer and consultant, and is writing a number of books for publication. He also is a full-time doctoral student at the University of Georgia.

His publications include the ACUHO-I *Talking Stick, Mind Mapping: A New Training Model* (October 2001) and articles in the *College Student Affairs Journal* (Spring 2000). Jon has also presented at SEAHO, ACUHO-I, and ACPA.

Acknowledgments

A number of very valuable people have helped in various ways to make this book possible. First, thank you to my family for their support, encouragement, and willingness to help me make this idea a reality. I appreciate all that you have done to help make this happen.

Second, thank you to Vicki Hawkins and the Department of University Housing at Georgia Southern University for providing me with the opportunity to attend the MBTI® training with the Center for the Application of Psychological Type in Gainesville, Florida. Discovering how much more there is to type theory was a major source of inspiration in realizing that the MBTI could be used for much more that I had ever realized or even considered.

Third, thank you to the student staff, both graduate and undergraduate, that I have worked with at Southern Illinois University at Carbondale, Georgia Southern University, and the University of Southern Mississippi. Being able to see in real life how the information and the mental state that the MBTI provides can improve one's relationships with people is what led to the idea that it is possible to apply the MBTI specifically to the residence-hall setting.

Finally, thank you to Norbert Dunkel for all his help in reviewing the material and providing feedback and input on its style and presentation, and for encouraging me to write and publish the work.

Cover photos courtesy of University of Maryland College Park. Cover design by George Peach Design of Columbus, Ohio.

Preface

Welcome to *RA Types*. This book is designed to give the reader a brief understanding of the theory behind the Myers-Briggs Type Indicator®. It is to be used primarily with Resident Assistants, Hall Directors, Area Directors, and anyone who works with the live-in staff of the residence halls.

The first chapter discusses the basics of type theory starting with a definition and the history of how it developed. Chapter 2 defines what is a preference and how does it manifest in the people that you interact with as well as what each of the preference pairs mean. After discussing each pair, Chapter 3 wraps up the basic concepts of type theory with a few thoughts about how the information discussed can be used in interactions with RAs.

The detailed descriptions of each of the 16 personality types described by the Myers-Briggs Type Indicator, as applied to the Resident Assistant position, begin in Chapter 4. Each section starts with a general description of that particular type, then goes on to how the type learns and the kinds of *Training* methods that they are most responsive to. A description of the preferred *Work Environment* and a discussion of the kinds of attitudes and people that they prefer to work with, as well as some thoughts on the kind of supervision that they need follows.

Following work style, the book describes the kind of *Leader* they are in a group or organization. How they get others to work, how they may take on a leadership role, and how they may prioritize issues or concerns are covered. *Programming* addresses the kinds of programs that they will prefer as well as how they respond to the expectations of the department.

How each type deals with *Organizational* issues is discussed in limited detail as some types have specific issues that affect their organizational skills. A discussion of the kinds of *Relationships with their Residents*, how they interact with the residents and establish friendships and connections, and the approach that they use towards building community for their floor follows.

Finally, each section describes any *Issues* or concerns that each type has to deal with in their life; addressing how some of their strengths can become weaknesses, as well as suggestions for development and warning signs that a supervisor should be aware and watch out for in their behavior.

Chapter 5 provides you with some sample exercises and activities that can be used with your staff, both individually and as a group.

A list of Internet and other resources that readers can use to further develop their own understanding of type theory and the MBTI is provided. In addition, the two main sources of information, resources, and support information about the MBTI are provided.

Finally, Chapter 6 closes with some final thoughts about this material and how to use it in the residence halls. I hope that the reader enjoys *RA Types* and hopefully find this book a useful resource.

Jon K. Coleman
University of Georgia
September 2003

History and Development
of Type Theory

History and Development of Type Theory ———————————

What is type theory? That is a question that is not easily answered without a great deal of background information, psychological history and terms, and in-depth study. This book will not go into great detail of these issues; rather it will discuss how type theory applies to working with Resident Assistants/Advisors or other student staff in the residence halls. Some of the history of how the Myers-Briggs Type Indicator® (MBTI) came about will be covered to help you understand the theory and be able to use the information in this book effectively. There are some key points that you need to keep in mind while considering the information that is described here. First, type theory relies on empirical evidence for its proof. There is no guarantee that it is 100% accurate or useful. What has been established is years of useful application on an international level with a large number of people. And while people have different views on how useful it is, type theory has provided its users with a great many tools for working with, counseling, supervising, and supporting the people around them.

Second, no theory about personality development is going to hold for all personality types simply because some of those types will resist any attempt at being categorized. People can be funny about anything that limits them and will seek to undermine the conclusions of those theories so that they will have beaten the system. The theory that the MBTI is based upon has proved to be fairly accurate in describing the 16 personality types and is used by many professionals in all areas of life. As a reader, you will have to determine the usefulness of this material.

Third, type theory is not about the individual's quality of work or ability level. The theory only tells you about the natural *tendencies* of a person: what is most comfortable for them, what they are most likely to depend upon in a stressful situation, and what they see as the right way of doing things. Each person will have experiences in their lives that will affect how their tendencies manifest. If they feel that what is natural for them is somehow wrong, or if they feel that they need to more fully develop the traits that they do not possess, then that person can work to develop those abilities and may seem to either possess them or want to possess them. A person who is not comfortable in social settings, preferring instead privacy or small groups, may feel that being outgoing and social is better, even though that is not natural for them. This book aims to help supervisors and their staff understand that the difference in personality types is a difference between two strengths, not between strength and weakness. Anyone with the determination to do well can achieve his or her goals with the proper support and environment. One personality type may be a natural leader for whom the exercise of authority is not only natural but also sought after. Another personality type may not normally look for the spotlight. However, type theory does not tell you which will do the better job, only which one will probably have an easier time.

History

To understand type theory, it helps to have an understanding of where it came from and how it developed. To start with, it is not some new idea that some business leader developed in the last few years to sell some books or to start his or her consulting business. The fundamental idea of type theory goes back to the ancient Greeks and was mentioned as early as 400 BC by Plato.[1] The idea was that there exists basic structures of personality in every person that could be described and used to understand them. Over the centuries, others (Aristotle, Paraclesus, Fromm, etc.) have also used this idea to try and explain how people think and behave. While there have been many reasons given and theories constructed for how these traits are developed, no consensus or proof exists that can be used in this work. If you are interested in this aspect of type theory, there is a great deal of material available to the interested researcher.

The next phase of the development of type theory was the idea of a single motivation for personality development. Early psychologists believed that people acted from a single underlying desire or need that shaped their behavior and motivations. While there was no agreement as to what this primal motivation was — for Sigmund Freud it was lust[2] — there was a general acceptance that all people shared the same motivation. Carl Jung offered a different interpretation of personality development. He felt that there were fundamental differences in people and what motivated their behavior. Jung's work was based on the idea that inside each person was a series of *archetypes,* a standard set of personality models that all people share, which drove their behavior. Although no particular *archetype* was better than another, there was one that was more natural or comfortable to that person and this shaped their individual personality.

Jung's theories did not gain much audience at the time until Isabel Myers and her mother Katherine Briggs, neither of whom were psychologists or physicians, came along and brought attention back to Jung's ideas. Isabel spent many years working with her own observations about people and, combining it with Jung's work, designed an instrument that would allow her to determine a person's personality type. Thus the Myers-Briggs Type Indicator was created. (*Note:* MBTI administrators do not use the word test because of the connotations of passing and failure that are associated with that word. It is more accurate to describe the MBTI as an instrument because it is used to measure the preferences of the person filling in the answers and to give a reading of their scores that can be used to determine that person's personality type. It is mostly a matter of semantics, but out of respect, this book will also use that language.)

Since the 1950s the MBTI has been in used in all manner of situations and circumstances. It has been used in business by managers trying to better understand their staffs, by counselors to improve communication between couples, by parents trying to understand their children, and by educators trying to better educate their students. People behave in ways that are the most natural and comfortable to them. External pressure can alter a person's natural tendencies, but it is rarely the cause of it. Type theory allows observers to see why a person behaves in a way that is deemed inappropriate, undesirable, or problematic. Society has determined that certain manifestations of personality are either good or bad depending on the circumstances or accepted norms. For example: extroverted personality traits (being outgoing and social) are often considered healthier than introverted (inwardly directed and reserved)

---

[1] Keirsey, David. (1998). *Please Understand Me II: Temperament, Character, Intelligence,* Del Mar, CA: Prometheus Nemesis Book Company

[2] Briggs Myers, Isabel and McCaulley, Mary H. (1985). *Manual: A Guide to the Development and Use of the Myers-Briggs Type Indicator.* Palo Alto, CA: CPP Inc.

ones. This may simply be that there are more extroverted types in the population and that they are more visible by their very nature, but whatever the reason there are different values given to different aspects of personality. Sometimes a trait's value can even vary in different circumstances.

Chapter

2

Preferences and Pairs

Preferences and Pairs

In order to understand what preference means in the real world, you need to understand what each type preference is trying to describe. A preference is simply a natural tendency to behave or believe in a certain way. It is the most comfortable response or action for a person that is unconcerned about what others think or believe. In many ways it is no different from preferring chocolate to vanilla ice cream, it is just a tendency that exists within each person.

The MBTI uses a system of preference pairs to describe each personality type. The preference pair is made up of two opposing concepts that address a particular concern or circumstance. Neither preference is right or better than the other, but rather they present different ways to approach the same concerns.

Exercise 2.1

To understand the difference, try signing your name on a piece of paper. Now try signing your name with the other hand. Does it feel any different? During the second attempt, you may find yourself having to think about how to spell your name, how to write a particular letter, or other issues that you never even thought of the first time. The end product probably does not look very much like your normal signature either. With time and practice, you could probably improve your efforts and maybe even make it look very nice, but it will never be as comfortable as the dominant hand. Preferences are like that as well. We learn to value the benefits of the other preference, but it will never be the norm for us.

Extroversion and Introversion

The first preference pair described is Extroversion and Introversion. This preference concerns how people focus their attentions and how they become stimulated and energized. Energy in this context refers to the emotional/mental motivation that allows a person to function at their best. It deals with the world that a person prefers to live and operate in as well as the world where they feel the most comfortable. This pair also describes how a person can become exhausted or burned out because the kind of activities that energize one preference will exhaust the other one.

For extroverted personalities, their focus is on the external world of people and things. It is directed outward from the person and they get their energy from their interactions with other people and things. They are stimulated by their interactions with others and this often manifests as an outgoing and social manner that puts them at ease in all manner of social situations. They enjoy being around others and will often fill their time with activities that allow them to coordinate, socialize, and function in groups. It often seems that they think out loud and this is a fairly accurate description, as they prefer to process information through interactions rather than reflection. They will often say things that may not be well thought out because they are using the discussion as a process to come to a decision. Extroverted personalities are often described as friendly, social, and easy to talk to. They are also very good at those activities that allow for social interactions and group effort such as brainstorming and icebreakers.

For introverted personalities, their focus is on the internal world of thoughts and ideas. They focus inwards and get their energy from being quiet and alone, or with a very select group of friends. They prefer to have time to consider questions and issues in their own mind before discussing it with others. While their opposite thinks aloud, they prefer to go over their thoughts and get them into a polished form before sharing them. This often gives them an intellectual air as they present ideas that are both well thought out and well developed, compared to the initial thoughts of the extroverted personality. They often will go through the same thought processes of the extrovert, but the difference is that others do not get to participate in or hear that process, so they appear to be more developed. Introverted types are often considered shy and reserved because of their views on socializing, whether that may or may not be the fact.

For this pair, activities that energize one will exhaust the other. For example, an extrovert will be motivated and energized by being around others, interacting with them, and being stimulated by the outside world. This may be a party, playing with a sports team, or going out for a night on the town. This, to an introvert, would be work. It drains their energies and wears them down. They need time alone, or with a very select group of friends, to recharge. The quiet time allows them to reflect on what is going on and digest it so that they are ready for more. But to the extrovert, having to spend time alone, quietly thinking is something that would wear them out.

For the RA position, the extrovert has an obvious advantage over the introvert. Because they are responsible for a floor of residents and they are dealing with those residents all of the time, they can maintain a high level of energy. Their outgoing nature makes them appear friendly and approachable and they usually are good about talking to residents, socializing with large groups of people, even when they do not know the people involved, and in being available to those around them. This allows them to establish bonds with their residents faster than introverts and while they may not have as much depth in their connections, others often do not realize this.

Introverted RAs will have to work to develop these skills. Because they need personal time away from others to recharge, they have to struggle to remember to do the things that their opposite does naturally. While it may not be natural for them, it does not mean that they are not capable of doing it. In fact, many introverts are able to function in a manner that makes others believe them to be extroverted because of the nature of their job. It is only when you examine their behavior in a broader view that you realize that their personalities are introverted. They may not enjoy the floor meetings, icebreakers, and other group activities, but they are likely to form deeper bonds over time with residents and fellow staff members, or at least with a few of them. In the general population there are 75% Extroverts and 25% Introverts[1]. Some words to emphasis each preference:

Extroverts: outward, social, wide ranging, active, many, people, things
Introverts: inward, private, deep, reflective, few, ideas, privacy

---

[1] Briggs Myers, Isabel and McCauley, Mary H. (1985), *Manual: A Guide to the Development and Use of the Myers-Briggs Type Indicator*. Palo Alto, CA: CPP Inc.

Sensing and Intuition

The second preference pair is Sensing and Intuition, which deals with the kinds of information that a person looks for and trusts the most to use in making decisions. While the first pair looked at whether a person focused on the internal or external world, this pair takes that world and shows how a person focuses either on the specifics, details, and current realities of that world or on the general view, patterns, themes, and future possibilities.

The sensing personalities focus on the specifics of their world. They look at the details and focus on what is real and in front of them. They seek and trust information that is relayed to them by their senses. If they cannot see, smell, touch, taste, or hear it, then it is not a fact. It is a guess and therefore not very reliable. Sensing personalities focus on the present. They deal with the real world right now. They are usually good with tools and physical activities that allow them to use their senses. While some personalities prefer a stable and solid existence (SJs), some prefer an existence that is full of opportunity, fun, and new adventures (SPs). But whatever the personal preference, the sensing type focuses on reality.

The intuitive personality prefers to look at the big picture. They enjoy understanding the underlying causes and principles that cause results. They focus on the future and trust their gut or hunches. They do not pay particular attention to details, as they do not consider them to be as important as the overall goal or picture. For the intuitive, it is the broad vision of what is possible and what is to come that draws them into a project or position. They are the ones who will see the potential within a person or a job and can work to make that potential real. The intuitive personality enjoys change as a process of discovering what works and how each piece of the puzzle interacts with the others. It is when they can be creators and innovators that they have the most enjoyment and enthusiasm for what they are doing. They are the beginners and starters of an organization's work, but they struggle to maintain the interest necessary to keep it going, preferring to rely on the sensors for that kind of work.

Both preferences bring value to a group or a team. From the sensors you get hard work, attention to details, and a commitment to ways of doing things that provides the stability to keep a group or organization functioning. They provide a group with a grounding in the real world and keep attention focused on what is happening right now so that the group does not spread out or become inattentive to the pressures and demands of day-to-day operations. From the intuitives, you get vision and inspiration. They are the motivated to challenge the establishment and the patterns of the past. They are able to foresee changes and new possibilities that are coming your way and can help to prepare the group to meet those challenges. They keep an organization fresh and ready to seize opportunities and keeps the group's attention focused on what is next, what they can be doing to improve and better themselves and the organization. In the general population, about 75% are Sensing and 25% are Intuitive.[2] Some words to describe both preferences:

Sensing: present, details, facts, specifics, tradition, repetition, literal, practical

Intuitive: future, patterns, potential, imagination, innovation, variety, change

---

[2] *Ibid.*

Thinking and Feeling

The third preference pair deals with how a person makes the decisions that guide their behavior and choices in their lives. Using the information that the second preference gives them, the third decides how that information will be utilized and weighed in making decisions for themselves and the group that they belong to. Of all the preference pairs, only this one has any statistically relevant correlations to another factor and that is gender. Thinking is favored by 60% of men in the population while feeling is favored by 65% of women.[3] Though it is not enough of a difference to make broad assumptions or generalities about a particular person, it allows for a comparison between what we view as stereotypically male and female behaviors of this preference pair.

The thinking personality uses information in a logical and rational way that favors objective reasoning and can be viewed as being impartial and even impersonal. They may weigh each piece of information before they come up with a solution or decision. Each piece of information that affects a decision — whether it involves cost, personal feelings, or long-range implications — is data to be considered in making a decision. The thinker is best associated with the head or the brain. This preference reasons out why a decision will be made with precise reasons and consequences. They are the looking for consistency and rationality in the world and prefer that others see their behavior as being consistent with a set of guiding principles.

The feeling personality sees information as having a value that influences not only how they feel, but also how it affects others. Relationships are primarily important to them as they create and maintain harmony within their life. Each piece of information that they receive has a particular value to them and the final combination of values will determine what choices they make based on the decision that has the best effect on everyone. The feeler is associated with the heart or feelings. This preference focuses on caring and appreciation of individuals and seeks to promote a sense of empathy in others. Decisions can be seen as inconsistent, but that is because the circumstances of each case are different and calls for different solutions. Like the thinker, the feeler also has a strong a set of principles, but this set is based on people, not facts. This counters the impersonal justice of the thinker with the considered mercy of the feeler. Some words to describe both preferences:

Thinker: head, objective, rational, principle, impersonal, logical, precise
Feeler: heart, subjective, personal, values, caring, empathy, harmony

Judging and Perceiving

The preference pair of Judgment and Perceiving deals with how a person prefers to order and operate in their environment as well as the goal of their decisions. This preference explains the goals or objectives of the person making the decisions and what he/she hopes to achieve. It also tells how they organize their energy in their interac-

———————————————
[3] *Ibid.*

tions with the world. The first preference pair tells whether a person prefers the internal or external world; the second tells whether the focus of that world is on specific details or on the big picture; and the third preference tells how people make decisions. This fourth preference tells whether the person gets satisfaction from completing tasks or from what is involved in the process of completing them, i.e., enjoying the journey more than the destination. This preference also gives you a good indication of the organizational skills and time-management priorities of the person and how they interpret and use those abilities.

The judging personality focuses on organization and completion. Their goal is to complete a task in the best and most deliberate manner. They seek to provide organization and structure to their world so that they have control over what is occurring around them, which allows them to know and plan for the tasks and responsibilities that they have. They are productive individuals who are very good with time-related tasks and usually manage to schedule themselves very well. They are likely to have and use planners or other methods to track their jobs, responsibilities, and appointments so that they are on time and are finished when they are supposed to be. As a rule, they are very aware of timeliness and bothered when it is lacking in others. The judging personality is a deliberate one that is not interested in the path to a particular solution, but the solution itself.

The perceiving personality loves flexibility and freedom. Their goal is to be able to respond and adapt to the changing world and not to be locked into a particular path or destination. They enjoy spontaneity and the ability to go with the flow. For them, it is not the completion of a task that is the ultimate goal, but rather it is the process of getting there. Discoveries along the way, new and unexpected surprises, and having an openness to the world around them means that they are able to take advantage of whatever comes their way. The perceiving preference is not concerned with time or organization and it usually shows up in their work. While they may strongly desire to be organized, and willing to invest the time and energy in starting new systems to make themselves more efficient, they rarely have the interest necessary to maintain those systems. It is not that they do not value organization, but that they value their ability to quickly respond to new situations more.

As with all of the preference pairs, this one provides strengths and difficulties for both an individual and a group. The judging preference provides organization and structure and a determination to finish the job. They will push to see things through as well as provide concrete results and have the discipline necessary to handle all of the different responsibilities that they have. The perceiving preference provides flexibility and adaptability that allows the group to take advantage of new situations and circumstances as well as providing a sense of adventure and excitement to what is happening. They are quick to adjust and do not struggle when changes to the plan occur that can paralyze the judging personalities.

Of all the preference pairs, this one is most likely going to be the source of conflicts and difficulties. They look at things so diametrically different that it is often hard to find common ground or shared values. This is especially true for following procedures, being on time, and following through on their job duties. The judging personalities need to work to recognize the value and benefits that the perceiving personality provides, and vice versa. In the general population, about 55-60% of people have the judging preference.[4] Some terms associated with each preference:

Judging: organization, structure, completion, control, deadline, results
Perception: flexibility, adaptability, freedom, spontaneity, process, experience

---

[4] *Ibid.*

Chapter
3

Using This Information

Using This Information

Within each person are certain traits and tendencies that are natural and most comfortable for them. *RA Types* tries to describe those tendencies as they relate to the RA position. However, it does not tell about the life experiences of a particular RA that can alter how those tendencies may manifest in his/her behavior. As mentioned in the beginning of the book, lifetime experiences, even as short as that of a traditional college student, can alter a person's values. An introvert who grew up as a very reserved, private, and quiet person may come to college with the determination that they need to be more outgoing and be willing to put themselves in social situations. As they do so, a casual evaluation of that person may result in the belief that they possess an extroverted personality; the truth is not so easily discovered without additional effort. It is critical to remember that while observation may provide a person with a good impression of someone's personality type, it may not necessarily be accurate.

So, having just limited everything that this book will describe, how is this material going to be of any use? Reading the descriptions of the 16 RA types will show that there are a number of conflicts that cannot be easily addressed or solved without tremendous effort. For example, in the area of training, each RA type often has different goals, objectives, preferred presentation styles, and desired outcomes. How can you design a training program that provides for the enthusiastic spontaneity that the ENFP wants with the structured style that the ISTJ prefers? There is no easy answer, but one begins by being aware of the different tools for training that exist which allow a presenter to reach out to each preferred style of learning.

To get the best use of this information, it is recommended that staff members first use the MBTI to assess their individual personality types. After that, a presentation can describe what the preferences mean and how to interpret their personal results. This allows the person the chance to see whether or not the MBTI accurately portrayed his/her preferences. Once the type for each staff member has been determined, then the material found here can be much more useful to a supervisor. If the instrument is not available, self-scoring is the next best method instead of the supervisor attempting to guess the different types of each staff member.

If having each staff member take the MBTI is not an option, then the preference pairs can be presented to the staff as part of a training session and each staff member can determine which pair is their type preference. If this is the method to be used, it is important that each preference is presented as fairly and evenly as possible. Presenters should also emphasize that each preference is both valuable and good, but that they are different and even if one likes the descriptions of both preferences, only one of them can be chosen. Some individuals will attempt to identify the preference that the presenter is favoring in order to find the most acceptable answer. Self scoring does not have to be elaborately or extensively presented; it just has to be delivered in such a manner that both types in each preference pair is demonstrated as being advantageous, valuable, and useful for the RA position.

The next step is to review the material for each individual staff member and design an individualized supervisory plan to work with each of them. This allows a supervisor to work with each staff member personally to develop those areas in which they may need work to work on so as to spotlight and take full advantage of their natural strengths and interests. It also helps them to be aware of any issues or tendencies that may affect the evaluation of their job performance. This will also allow the supervisor to see the degree of supervision that their staff may need and/or want.

Designing an Individual Supervisory Plan

Creating a method to supervise a staff member or group of staff requires the supervisor to distill down the information in each RA Type to how the staff member deals with issues relevant to their position, department goals, and the supervisor's leadership style. The first step is to create a profile for the supervisor. This will allow him/her to identify his/her own issues, strengths, and tendencies and how they relate to his/her work in the residence halls.

For example, supervisors with the ESTJ type will have some of the following aspects to their leadership style. They have an outgoing personality and are not only organized but also natural leaders. They work best in an environment where logic and reason dictate and consistency is a key operating philosophy. Timeliness is not only part of their nature, but also a sign of respect. They operate in a hierarchical structure that makes sense to them and while they can be driven and tough, they get results.

Knowing this information about themselves, ESTJ supervisors will be able to anticipate future conflicts and difficult issues that they may have with their Introverted, Intuitive, Feeling, or Perceptive staff members. This will allow them to determine where they can be proactive and find ways to bring their differing values together. The ESFP RA, for example, will relate very well on issues of socialization, teambuilding, and training methods. The conflicts will more likely manifest in meeting deadlines, making it to meetings on time, and emphasis on the relationships of the group. If people are unhappy, then the ESFP does not work well and will want to spend time dealing with the issues. The ESTJ supervisor who remains focused on the tasks can demotivate this RA. A sample Individual Supervision Plan is displayed in Figure 3.1

Figure 3.1 Sample plan for ESFP RA

Individual Supervision Plan for _____

Training
- Prefers practical training, not a great deal of theory
- Be clear and precise in explaining what is required
- Enjoys being able to practice new skills or tasks
- Best when working with others in groups or teams
- Learns best when they feel connected to the presenter

Work Environment
- Likes an exciting visual workplace
- Focuses on people and relationships
- Deals with the present and needs of the moment
- Likes to contribute ideas and thoughts to operations and methods
- Needs harmony between staff

Leadership
- Spontaneous, able to respond to sudden changes and surprises
- Great representative of the organization/department
- Wants everyone to be involved
- Good as a mediator/peacemaker
- Good crisis manager
- Wants to participate in guiding the group, need to have input

Programming
- Knows their residents to find best programs for floor
- Good with spontaneous programs
- Struggles with advance planning
- Struggles with administrative details

Organization
- Struggles with time management
- Struggles with organization
- Tools need to be immediately useful or they are ignored
- Explain needs of procedures as how absence affects others

Relationships
- Spends a great amount of time and energy on good relationships
- Good at meeting and interacting with others
- Empathetic to others
- May accept surface explanations for behavior and not look beyond
- Perceptive of issues developing between others

Issues
- Can socialize so much that they forget to do the job required
- Wants to be friends with residents, even if it keeps them from doing the job
- New things can distract them from current projects/responsibilities
- Needs to work on their follow through
- Learns to prioritize efforts and time
- Learns to think and plan ahead, not jump into things

Chapter 4

RA Type Descriptions

RA Type Descriptions

ISTJ The Dutiful RA	ISFJ The Helping RA	INFJ The Idealistic RA	INTJ The Designing RA
ISTP The Problem-Solving RA	ISFP The Caring RA	INFP The Perfectionist RA	INTP The Analyzing RA
ESTP The Hummingbird RA	ESFP The Social RA	ENFP The Adventurous RA	ENTP The Competitive RA
ESTJ The Planning RA	ESFJ The Assessing RA	ENFJ The Humanistic RA	ENTJ The Executive RA

The ISTJ Resident Assistant:
The Dutiful RA

The ISTJ RA is best described by the words responsibility, duty, consistency, and reliability. These RAs are aware of the duties and responsibilities and works to complete them, often putting personal and academic concerns as a lower priority in order to make sure that the work is done. Very organized and time aware, they are great at scheduling and handling the different aspects of the job, but they shine most in dealing with administrative tasks.

Reserved and seemingly a bit aloof, ISTJs holds their feelings and beliefs close to the chest, letting few see inside. They value what works, which is proven by experience and actual hands-on proof. They deal well with an established structure and a hierarchical system that follows a traditional way of doing things.

Training

ISTJs respond best to training that is practical, no-nonsense, and hands on. They do not trust fun experiences. They are able to apply the information best when they see the training as being practical and useful. Paperwork, filling out forms, and other types of responsibilities that leave little or no room for invention appeals to them as they see the procedures as reliable and trustworthy.

ISTJs don't value theoretical work that is not immediately practical and useful, and will tolerate it only when it leads to concrete ends. Their preference for a step-by-step approach causes them to shy away from training that emphasizes intuitive leaps, unstructured situations, or free-flowing association. They want to know what Step 1 is before going on to Step 2, and so forth.

ISTJs expect their training materials to be correct and error-free. Finding errors in the material makes them cautious of what is being presented and strengthens a belief in greater errors that have not been discovered. Information that is specific to their job must be correct; just the presence of errors will make learning difficult for them. Their respect for authority is strong until the authority shows flaws, then their trust and belief quickly fades.

Activities that benefit the ISTJs need to be designed to allow proper time for reflection about the materials so that they can process the information. They enjoy being able to think about what is being taught before being expected to buy into the training or to express their opinion. These RAs have a strong sense of separation from work and play and the two need to stay that way. Following a published schedule, starting and stopping on time, and making clear distinctions between what they are required to do and what is optional, allows them to trust the presenters and, therefore, the presenter's information. Hands-on activities that allow them to actually do a task or perform a job reinforces the learning and supports their appreciation of the work being done.

Work Environment

ISTJs can be viewed as the clock of an organization. Timely, purposeful, and preferring work to relationships, they are often the grounding force in any group. They are practical and view themselves as realists and may encounter difficulty in dealing with activities designed to let things flow, i.e., brainstorming. They value practicability and the use of established procedures and ways of doing things.

Time is a crucial element for the ISTJ RAs. If a meeting is supposed to start at 9:00, they feel that starting at 9:01 is late. Keeping to a schedule, whether beginning or ending a meeting, working on an event, or their personal life is a source of stability and certainty in their world. This sense of control and reliability allows them to feel comfortable in what is happening around them. As long as they feel that their planner is accurate, then the world is right. Constant plan changes or sudden expectations will upset them, even though they may not express it.

They also need to see concrete and tangible results from their efforts. If you tell them to produce three programs, they will come up with three programs although they may not come up with creative and amazing ones. The need for exact expectations can be difficult when trying to allow them freedom to assess the needs of their floor. If you tell ISTJs to do "whatever programs their floor needs" but their residents tell them that they do not need any, they feel that they have done their job. They are the ultimate literalists!

Recognition for continuous work is valued on a regular basis. Praise for motivation's sake is counterproductive. They give recognition towards another person's efforts only when that work exceeds normal expectations. Doing the job that the person was hired to do is not grounds for reward; it is the agreement that was made when they took the job.

ISTJs have a strong sense of responsibility and loyalty to their organization, especially to a superior who has proven to be capable. They value traditions and time-honored ways of doing things, especially if those traditions reflect their own views.

Surprisingly, they are usually quick to embrace ideas that support traditions (holiday party, sporting event activities, hall traditions, etc.) even if the activity is not one they would normally enjoy. Honoring the history and ways of the past holds a special place in their heart.

The ISTJ Leader

The leadership development of ISTJ RAs is usually not the result of their planning, but from being recognized for their strengths and abilities by others and being encouraged to become a leader. Highly competent in their activities, ISTJs rise to positions of responsibility due to their reliability, stability, and consistency in performing their tasks. They will take on the role of a leader more for their feeling of being able to do the job right than from any desire to hold a position of authority, make friends, meet people, or some other motivation.

ISTJs are very task oriented and can often overlook or outright ignore the relationship side of the equation. In their pursuit of accuracy in their tasks, they can be perceived as uncaring, rigid, or dictatorial. They do not desire control over anyone else, rather it is their desire for things to be done right from the start that causes them to shut out all other factors. Once everything is functioning correctly, then they can deal with other matters.

One area where this natural tendency is softened is when the RA has had a supervisor who they viewed as successful and did things right. They often mimic behaviors that they saw that person doing, not because they agree with the internal reasons; rather they feel that they should do it as well because the supervisor was successful. This allows them to bring in relationship-building activities such as birthday parties or other fun things for the group, but always at the appropriate time and place.

This trait, while positive in many respects, can be negative when dealing with new leadership situations. With their strong sense of history and way of doing things, the ISTJ can be hard on a new supervisor or system. "That's not the way we do it" or other similar comments from them would not be unusual, especially if they had a strong sense of loyalty to previous supervisor. On the other hand, a new supervisor who is replacing one that did not meet their expectations may get a great deal of support, especially if the new supervisor meets their expectations. Asking these RAs for their input and assistance in creating procedures for the staff utilizes their experience and preferences for the group's benefit.

ISTJs have a strong sense of fairness and they want to be perceived as objective, fair, and impersonal decision makers. Not one to be swayed by emotional issues, they have a strong sense of justice and feel it should be applied with an even hand. During confrontations, they will rely heavily on established rules and procedures and are least likely to substitute their personal judgment.

The ISTJ leaders are traditionalists, stabilizers, and consolidators. They deal well with repetitive tasks, taking comfort in knowing and doing exactly what is expected.

Programming

The ISTJ programmers are also very much the traditionalists. They see the requirements in a very quantitative manner and are not going to program off the cuff.

Most likely to plan their activities logically and methodically, they balance academic demands, personal issues, and other factors when scheduling their events. While not being the most creative type, they are among the most consistent.

They struggle most in dealing with ambiguous expectations. Clear definitions of the types and numbers of programs cause them the least stress and increase their sense of stability and loyalty to their supervisor. They know what is expected of them from the beginning and can act accordingly. They deal very poorly with changes midstream unless there is absolutely no doubt that the change is necessary.

Organization

ISTJs are probably the most organized of all types, but they are rarely satisfied with their own organizational skills. Using files, notebooks, and orderly locations of material, they are the consummate office keepers. They prefer a very hands-on approach that demonstrates its logic and simplicity to everyone who sees it. They are able to adapt to the needs of their subordinates (whether residents or junior staff) as long as the overall source of control remains theirs.

Relationship with Residents

ISTJs are not going to be the "rah-rah cheerleaders" on the staff. Reserved in their manner, they are more likely to stick with tried and true friends and do not make new friends easily. They see themselves as a source of information, policy, and authority for the floor rather than as the new best friend of the residents (as some types will). Their reserve is often mistaken for indifference, especially by the extroverts, and can easily cause misunderstandings and difficulties.

These RAs need to make special efforts to reach out more and be seen as someone beyond the enforcer of the rules. They will usually establish a good rapport with residents in the long run, but it will be a gradual process that others are usually unaware of.

In dealing with residents, ISTJ RAs have one very strong asset going for them and that is their sense of fair play and consistency. They are not viewed as playing favorites with residents or enforcing policies arbitrarily. They are usually viewed as tough but fair in their dealings and meaning exactly what they say. This bluntness can be difficult to some, but it is critical to the sense of responsibility of the ISTJ RA.

Issues of Concern

Various areas of concern need to be addressed with this type. First is their tendency to isolate themselves from others. Their introverted tendencies and sense of righteousness makes them appear as unfriendly or antisocial. The reality is that they are very focused and driven, and prefer to have all work responsibilities out of the way before engaging in any fun or play. They do not deal well with failure, or even worse sloppiness, and their sense of responsibility also causes them to be perceived as being judgmental. Finally, ISTJs have a strong preference for a few friends that they develop over the years. It takes them a while to warm up to someone new and may take a significantly longer period of time before that person can be classified as a friend.

Others can view them as rigid, inflexible, and too focused on details. Their strong sense of what is appropriate can limit their interactions, especially when dealing with items that are not easily broken down into simple numbers or procedures. Because of this attention to detail, they often ignore the bigger picture. By focusing on their day-to-day responsibilities and actions, they can be blind to the long-range implications of their, or another's actions.

ISTJs are seen as one of the most reliable and dependable kinds of people in any group. As a result, they are often given, or take on, additional responsibilities because of how well they handle them. They often keep adding to that burden until they burn themselves out from overload. Their desire to make sure something is done right can cause them to distrust other people's abilities to do the job and makes them very hesitant to delegate responsibilities to others.

Change, especially those that comes from the outside, is another area of difficulty for the ISTJ RA. While willing to endorse changes that they feel are necessary to meet their sense of logic and common sense, they are quick to resist changes that they don't understand or see as valuable. Quick to fall back on traditional ways of doing things, they often ignore innovation in favor of familiarity. Changing expectations or procedures partway through the job upsets their sense of organization.

Dealing with ISTJ RAs means recognizing their pragmatic worldview instead of seeing them as pessimists. ISTJs often focus on what won't work in a scenario before giving the possibility of success any chance. This tendency towards pessimism increases as they become more stressed, and this stress is further increased in environments of constant change and the loss of the grounding ways of doing things that they prefer.

The ISTP Resident Assistant: The Problem Solving RA

The ISTP RAs are the problem-solvers of the group and like their ISTJ counterparts their strength lies in their ability to deal with facts, details, and logical reasoning. The difference lies in the fact that the ISTP enjoys a sense of freedom and a preference that shies away from the structure and schedules of the ISTJ. Enjoying the opportunity to truly experience life, they take great joy in being a part of the world around them by stimulating their senses. They seek to have their senses stimulated by very active activities and they enjoy those things that allow them to use those basic senses. ISTP RAs greatly enjoy using tools and physical equipment and demonstrate a great deal of ability in the use of those tools.

ISTP RAs seek out answers and understanding about how things work. Tinkerers at heart, they are likely to take something apart in order to see how it works. They possess great observation skills about the world around them, and their sense of flexibility gives them the ability to respond quickly and easily to needs without feeling disturbed. In fact they usually enjoy the sudden surge of stimulation that is provided by a crisis as it allows them to use the skills and knowledge they possess.

Training

The ISTP RAs are great at dealing with and incorporating factual, numerical, and logical information. Disdaining the theoretical fields, ISTPs seek out fields that are logical and make sense to their worldview. Information that is presented to them should be both concrete and useful, or else it is a waste of their time. If they can't use it, it is worthless.

The ISTPs enjoy getting their hands on things; however they also need time to sit back and reflect on what they have seen and done. They learn best when they have the ability to sit back and observe a demonstration, especially in a one-on-one setting. This part of their nature allows them to do very well during training for a mid-year replacement position as they do not need the full range of activities typically associated with the fall term. While they won't get the group interactions and dynamics that normally accompany training programs, this doesn't affect their ability to deal with the information and training. Information presented to them has to have a logical basis and reason. They produce best when they are allowed to work on projects that need systematic solutions, rather than ones of many possibilities. For them, there is one single answer and if that is not the case, then it is not a good question. They prefer to move at their own speed and learn on their own. They do not enjoy the group learning experience unless it allows them to apply competition and strategy. Activities that require the use or development of a strategy can engage them quicker. They like the challenge of competition and the opportunity to out-maneuver an opponent. While they may be pragmatic in their nature, ISTPs are gamblers at heart and are willing to take risks in the pursuit of their interests.

If the subject can be applied to their personal interests, then ISTPs can absorb huge quantities of information. For example, an ISTP interested in money and finance may be able to remember details and facts about budgets, expenses, costs, etc. for the group to such an extent that he will quickly become a dependable resource for others, a walking record book. On the other hand, if the subject does not interest him, then he will struggle with the material.

The ISTP does not give a special value to the presenter or teacher just because of their position. The only value they place on such people are on what they can teach them to do. Individual subjects do not really matter to the them, only how the information can be applied so that they can increase their understanding and use that information to further those interests.

ISTPs are very curious people who seek details, facts, and other information that interests them. They are able to remember large amounts of information and can usually recall it quickly and accurately.

Work Environment

ISTPs are independent workers. They prefer the freedom to do things their own way with the overall goals and objectives clearly defined. Rules are not critical or very important to them, as they will ignore them in favor of ease or efficiency. They want the projects that they are responsible for to be set out, but how they get there is where their independence and freedom will reign. Task-oriented, these RAs can easily ignore relationships and the feelings of other people. Not meaning offense, ISTPs simply see those issues as superfluous and therefore irrelevant to the job.

They greatly enjoy physical activities. Activities that allow them to really feel the moment that they are in provide them with the greatest level of stimulation. Not planners for tomorrow or dwelling on yesterday, ISTPs focus on the now. Unlike the ISTJs, they do not enjoy the routines of life and seek out new ways to stimulate their senses. Given a standard weekly task, ISTPs will seek to do it differently almost every time just to keep them interested.

ISTPs have a very strong desire for their personal freedom especially from authority — whether from a supervisor or from standard policies and procedures. They are hampered by the presence of any but the loosest command structures and despise operating within someone else's schedule.

Their remarkable ability to work with physical tools or items — vehicles, computer equipment, sports items, etc., — is manifested due to their desire to know and to be able to use all things. ISTP RAs enjoy the manipulation of things and knowing not only how to use them but how to use them better than others. Using these tools requires the full use of their senses and that is when they are at their finest.

The ISTP Leader

ISTP RAs lead primarily by example. They do what they think needs to be done and enjoy the action of doing things. The sense of right now is a theme that carries through all aspects of their life. They give others the information necessary to do their job but expect others to do it without supervision or oversight. A great delegator, ISTPs expect the same from their leader. A loose management style with the freedom to do things their own way will result in the best response from them. While needing this freedom, ISTPs must be cautious in their tendency to avoid schedules to such an extent that they miss crucial commitments.

ISTP RAs are a great source of strength and security in the face of adversity and crisis. Their ability to respond to change and surprise allows them to function well when they experience a sudden deviation from the norm. Their knowledge, calmness, self-confidence, and air of "I know what I'm doing" allow them to reassure others and manage the crisis in the most appropriate manner. In a crisis, it is their voice calling for order, calm, and for others to relax because things are under control. This is meat-and-drink to them because it allows them to focus only on the immediate moment, and they don't know what the next moment will bring. They are at their best in situations that require immediate attention. They are great at dealing with the situations that arise during RA duty but may not be as great at doing the duty rounds on time.

Programming

The type of programs that ISTP RAs provide closely follow their own personal interests. Programs that spotlight physical activities, like intramurals or other games, appeal to their senses. They are very adept at producing spontaneous programs as it appeals to their desire for freedom. Too much structure or control from a supervisor over how they do their programs often leads them to lose interest in doing any programs. Too many rules and policies to deal with will turn them off. Personal hobbies and interests will also manifest in their program efforts. For example, an ISTP who is interested in computers will likely seek to apply her knowledge and understanding of computers to her programming requirement. This allows them to not only showcase their own personal knowledge of the topic, but also enjoy the program themselves. Whether others enjoy it is not as critical an issue as whether they enjoy the presentation. Making connections through common interests is how they create their relationship with the residents.

ISTPs are able to combine work and play easily and enjoy it most when their work is play. They often drift into careers that allow their personal interests to match. Similarly, they believe programming should be fun. This allows them to get into the spirit of it. When they are having fun, they are masters of invention. Flights of fancy still elude them, but coming up with activities that are useful, logical, and unstructured will emerge from their efforts.

Organization

ISTP RAs are very haphazard at organization. While able to create masterworks of organization for their personal interests and hobbies, they tend to ignore the rest of their life. Able to find the best way to showcase a collection, organize a prize set of files, or other needs of their hobbies, they do not have the patience or interest in applying those skills to anything else. However, their sense of logic and rationality often provides them with a stability that others can interpret as organization.

As with the other perceiving types, the ISTP is not a time-conscious person. Time is not a function of their lives and they often just do not pay attention to it. Being late is not a critical issue unless it affects their ability to enjoy something. If being late to a game means that they cannot play then they will be on time. Otherwise, it is pretty much hit or miss. The same relaxed attitude applies to their expectations of others. They are less likely to be disturbed by someone else's tardiness, even though it may cause distress among other people in the group.

Relationship with Residents

Like most introverts, ISTPs are not going to be the social butterfly of any group. It will take time and conscious efforts for them to develop relationships with others, including their residents. One advantage is that when they are responsible for a group, they are more likely to make very individual efforts to meet, know, and keep up with the people that they are responsible for. They may be distant from other staff and residents, but with their own they usually do fairly well. Their best way of developing relationships with others comes from sharing information about common interests. An ISTP who is an avid basketball fan will likely amaze others with his/her almost computer-like recall of wins, losses, percentages, and past performance of teams and individuals.

ISTPs are also great observers. They are particularly observant of their environment and seem to have a great deal of insight into how people say they behave and the reality of that behavior. Noticing the difference between the beliefs and the reality of the actions of others, they rarely miss these differences and can provide dead-on critiques of those who fall short of their own perceived abilities.

Issues of Concern

ISTPs have a strong desire for personal free time to pursue their own interests. Because of this, they often take short cuts and avoid what is, to them, the unnecessary or boring parts of their job. This can result in others seeing them as either careless or unmotivated when, in fact, they are just so focused on getting back to their own personal interests. ISTPs are likely to change careers or majors when their current work or study no longer coincides with their personal interests.

Like most introverts, ISTPs can often be viewed as standoffish or unfriendly due to their sense of reserve, a lack of ease in social settings, and their desire to contemplate information before sharing their thoughts. They are slow to warm up to others and will need to get to know others on a very individual basis. They often maintain those connections past their term of employment, especially with those who share their interests. They need to learn to be more open and willing to share their thoughts with others. Often when they do share, they tend to focus on what's wrong with something rather than on the positive aspects of the situation. Their tendency towards pragmatism is often interpreted as pessimism.

Their sense of freedom and desire not to impose structure or control on others can result in a lack of communication with people they are responsible for. They can often hold back information that can help others simply because they do not want to be seen as controlling or providing too many rules. While great at delegating work assignments, they have trouble keeping up with those whose efforts they must coordinate. Their desire for freedom, from superiors and subordinates, can cause them to ignore others when they are not doing the necessary work or when others may need assistance and have not learned to ask for it yet.

Finally, their enjoyment of the pressure of time to inspire their creativity can cause them to engage in one of the most common issues for all of the perceiving types: procrastination. Waiting till the last moment may give them a charge in doing their work, but they need constant reminders about not putting things off due to the chance that something may come up and interrupt their last-minute work. Waiting right until when something is due and then having an emergency is not a justifiable situation; it is the result of poor management of their time. You have to walk the line with these ISTPs as their adaptability and free spirit makes them great at dealing with sudden changes but bad at the normal day-to-day expectations.

The ESTP Resident Assistant:
The Hummingbird RA

ESTPs are outgoing, practical, and realistic about life. Their preference for extroversion means that they are very comfortable in social settings and when combined with the perceptive preference they tend to think on their feet. Not one for planning ahead or contemplating things, thought and action are often simultaneous for ESTPs. This trait translates into a person who is usually lively, fun, and entertaining for the rest of the group, but the reason for their zest is entirely for themselves and not for others.

They seek to get the most out of life and enjoy all kinds of activities that allow them to fully experience life. High risk equals high reward.

Quick and flexible, ESTP RAs thrive in situations and environments that allow them exercise their ability to adjust rapidly to changing situations. They want to be where the action is and want to be a full part of anything that is happening. This can sometimes cause them to push some buttons when things are getting too boring for them. While not malicious, their behavior can stress the group in their desire for more action.

ESTP RAs are direct, often to the point of bluntness, but they respond equally well to clear thinking and talking. The curves that they encounter in their life do not disturb them. They tend toward activities that allow them the independence to do things in their own way and in their own time.

They are stimulated by their senses like the hummingbird is stimulated by the colors of the flowers in a garden. They are quick moving and react quickly to changes in their situation. Full of energy and enthusiasm, they often seem to be in constant motion and activity.

Training

ESTPs are curious about life and work and enjoy learning about how things work and function. Like the other STs, they prefer concrete and practical learning that avoids theoretical concepts. The ESTP learns best in an environment that emphasizes hands-on activities, directly applicable skill development, and sample exercises. They also enjoy the dynamics of the group and do well in learning settings that allow for interaction with other people and equipment.

Their grasp of concepts does not reflect well in testing or other standard ways of measuring learning. They demonstrate their understanding in actual situations where they can put their learning into place. This is one of the types that will really enjoy the mock role-plays such as "Behind Closed Doors." The opportunity to demonstrate their skills and understanding works much better for them than trying to write about what they have learned.

ESTPs do not function well in situations where they have to sit still for too long. They need to be moving and the presenter needs to engage them on a regular basis or they will be lost. Their focus is on the active, and the worst kind of teaching for them is the lecture. It requires continuous attention to someone who is not actively engaging them and that bores them.

Their learning sharply increases when the subject touches on something that matches their own interests. They are people-focused, practical and realistic, and prefer spontaneity to planning. They like to be entertained while learning as they associate their satisfaction with the learning experience with the level of acceptance and retention of the material being presented. They will be a different staff member the second year when they can bring the experiences of being an RA to the training. The second time around they can see where some of the material that is presented is not only relevant but also very useful. Until then they can be difficult in training sessions that do not meet their needs.

Work Environment

ESTPs work best in an environment that is filled with lively people who are focused on action. They prefer to work with people who value firsthand experience. They do not value a hierarchical structure, preferring a more free-flowing organization that allows them the freedom to do things their way. They also focus on more realistic and measurable organizational goals and results. Quantity of services is a great measure for them; trying to determine quality is too subjective to make an impact on them.

ESTPs need flexibility in their job performance as it feeds their need to be free of control. They like a space that looks nice and pleasant, something that is attractive to the senses. They need to have their five basic senses stimulated to be charged and ready to go. They enjoy a work setting that appeals to that part of their personality and take pride in how others see them.

ESTPs need a sense of compromise and movement to feel successful. They do not like inactivity, whether it is for planning or reflection, and they probably have difficulty in evaluation procedures as their preference is to keep going forward and not to look back. While STJs may focus on the past and the traditions that it represents, STPs are focused on the present. The needs of the moment is what is important and they can fail to meet set obligations, such as meetings or reports, if something comes up that needs their attention. Whether that something could have waited is not the issue, the issue is dealing first with what is right in front of them.

The ESTP Leader

ESTPs use their personal connections to persuade others to their way of thinking and doing things. Able to respond quickly to a crisis, they are great at dealing with the unexpected. Their major difficulty lies in the long-term planning of projects and activities that require a great deal of preparation. The ESTP can become bored quickly when results are not immediately apparent. They are direct and assertive in their dealings with others and are not shy about voicing their thoughts and opinions.

They are the "doers" of the organization and have a great willingness to jump into a situation with both feet running before they hit the ground. Their quickness and ability to adapt to what is going on around them allows them to deal with surprises with relative ease and comfort. Routine activities like meetings, publicity, reports, etc. can, however, cause them difficulty and result in others viewing them as lazy or uninterested. They are uninterested in those particular parts of the job.

Programming

ESTPs are the best spontaneous programmers. Their flexibility allows them to be able to put something together at the drop of a hat, and their relationships with others will usually result in good attendance. They favor programs that are active and physical or are practical and useful. Learning about your credit history and keeping it up isn't as appealing as learning about keeping your checkbook up and accurate. Both of those programs though would probably pale besides a physical game that allows them to use all of their senses.

Evaluation, assessment, and planning are areas that ESTPs need assistance in to overcome their own natural inertia. Their focus on right now causes them to ignore yesterday and not worry about tomorrow. They are able to produce programs for their residents that meet the requirements, but they will not be the ones to design new and outrageous concepts. Set clear expectations for them, but give them some freedom in how to make it work. Allowing them a degree of spontaneity will greatly improve their job perceptions.

Organization

The ESTP is not one of the most organized types. Like the rest of those with the perceiving preference, ESTPs have a very fluid sense of time and enjoy starting new things more than actually completing a task that they have started. Their focus on what is happening right now can cause them to miss appointments or, more likely, to be late. While this is upsetting to those of the judging preference, ESTPs don't consider lateness to mean anything; it is just that something has distracted them.

They tend to organize things as they go along and do what is the most expedient for the moment. For them, the phrase "it's better to ask forgiveness than to ask for permission" is a guiding principle. Their ability to make things work in the moment lets them believe that when confronted by their behavior, the results that they achieve should outweigh any other factors, even the set procedures and ways of doing things that they knew about, and just did not want to bother with.

The ESTP is not one to evaluate partway through a project, as it will usually result in a very poor evaluation. As they are working on something, there is chaos and lack of structure that others often cannot get a grip on. However, once complete, the final product will usually look good and meet the outlined needs. This is another example of how their need for freedom and independence manifests itself.

Relationship with Residents

Their extroversion preference means that the ESTPs will be able to deal with other people fairly easily. They are quick to make friends and though most of their relationships may be shallow, they usually have a great number of friends. They can easily talk with others and enjoy the opportunities for socialization that the RA position provides. They usually have a good grasp of what is going on with their residents, but they may not spend the necessary time and energy to see beyond the public faces of their residents and can miss some of the personal issues facing them. While they possess good powers of observation, those perceptions tend to focus on what is easily seen and detected. Their intuitive abilities are usually not very developed and they may need more information before being able to notice some of the more subtle concerns that are affecting their residents.

Their sense of fun and flexibility can create a sense of community and connection among the residents fairly easily. Their ability to improvise and respond to the moment can result in many activities with their residents that may never end up on a report or program form, but the residents will know about them.

Issues of Concern

Like all types, ESTPs have issues and areas that they need to be aware of and try to improve upon. Their tendency towards bluntness can cause hurt feelings and create rifts in their relationships with others. They need to be more aware of the human side of their dealing and how others feel. By showing more consideration for the feelings of others and reducing their own assertive tendencies, they can improve their relationship with those who are less likely to challenge their authority.

Planning is a major area of work for the ESTP. Their need for the quick fix may result in a temporary solution, but it is rarely the best one and will usually result in problems arising later. Their preference for improvisation may make them the life of the party, but they need to rely on it less in their work because it will catch up with them. Looking ahead and trying to determine what will work best in the long run is a skill that they will need. For example, a roommate conflict may cause them to want the residents moved because that will solve the problem with the least effort on their part. They often do not consider the need for both roommates to develop social, communication, and coping skills.

The ESTP sees school, whether college or before, as a place where friends meet and have fun. They tend to get caught up in their activities and their studies can easily suffer from neglect. Developing relationships with others and being engaged is their meat and drink; the class work is the price that they have to pay to get into the party.

Their sense of freedom allows them to join and leave groups easily as their interests change. Choosing careers and majors are usually as much the result of chance as they are of any great desire. They are able to move in and out of organizations without a great deal of personal difficulty and when that group no longer holds their interest, it is time to go. They need to be given the opportunity to apply their strengths in the free manner they prefer — at least some of the time if you are going to keep them happy, productive, and, if possible, focused.

ESTPs can demonstrate an amazing ability to spend a great deal of time and effort learning how to avoid problems and get ahead. Looking for short cuts and knowing all the rules allows them the ability to move ahead of others and draw attention and praise to themselves. This tendency directs them to understand the rules so they know which ones are really rules and which ones they can safely bend or break in the pursuit of their goals.

The ESTJ Resident Assistant:
The Planning RA

The ESTJ RA is a pragmatic planner and one of the most natural leaders. Combining a reasoned and logical approach to life with an outgoing personality and a strong sense of organization, the ESTJ meets most classic ideas of what a leader is all about. They have a strong need to be in charge and quickly rise to positions of leadership in the groups in which they belong. They are the doers of the group and are happy when they can roll up their sleeves and immediately start on the work at hand.

The ESTJ RA is a deliberate and determined worker who not only does well planning out a strategy for his/her projects, but is also good at following up. Closure is very important to ESTJs and they achieve that closure through the completion of the tasks that are set for them. Accountability is a major issue and they are just as quick to hold themselves and others to a high level of accountability. They are strong at monitoring the progress of those around them and keeping up with what everyone is supposed to be doing.

They are natural organizers and good at taking charge of situations. They work hard and have a competitive spirit in their play. They are strong believers in traditions and give them special credence. Holidays, birthdays, achievements, and other events that meet that historic or time-honored status are very important and must be paid attention to. Though often seemingly serious about what is going on around them, don't mess with the ways things are supposed to be.

Their sense of logic and reason acts as the guiding force in their lives. What is right is what works and if it doesn't work, or make sense to them, then they don't see reason to do it, even if it is the rule. Why obey rules that don't make sense? If it is working, then leave it alone. They do not handle change well, and messing up their routine is a capital offense. If changes must occur, you need to share the reasons with them or they will be mentally unbalanced by the upset to their sense of right and wrong. To them, life is in the details and you need to remember that!

Training

Like the other sensing types, the ESTJ prefers training that is heavy on the practical and useful and light on the theoretical. They want to know exactly what they are learning and what it is that they need to master the material being presented. Give them a step-by-step approach and stick to it. Schedules are important to them so if you say that you will be over at 9:15, don't go till 9:20. Even though they may not have anywhere else to go, you have to follow the schedule that you set.

ESTJs like to get their hands on what they are learning and wants to only study, listen, or read long enough to get started. When they encounter a problem, then its time to go back and learn more. They want the details and prefer situations that are both structured and have clearly defined goals and expectations, and they will probably grasp the administrative tasks quickly.

When you want ESTJs to agree with what you are showing them, you need to present clear, logical reasons backed up with facts. Sharing opinions or personal experience is not a real fact. Their experiences however are not only trustworthy but also reliable. They need things that are consistent and reliable to operate at their best and struggle with esoteric concepts or situations where the expected response is not clear. ESTJs may struggle with the counseling aspects of the job.

ESTJs enjoy working or studying with a group, but it needs to be organized. Free-flowing processes do not capture their attention and they are more likely to decide that they can do better on their own or with a more committed group. They like to see ideas that are put into practice and will get a great deal out of role-play situations and mock exercises. Giving them the chance to apply their learning directly or to be able to go on until they encounter a problem appeals directly to their nature.

Finally, the ESTJ is an active learner. They really enjoy getting into the specifics of a situation and looking at all of the details and facts but have difficulty putting it together to get the overall meaning. They can see the trees, but the forest eludes them. Their intense focus can also hamper their learning when they become so involved in the activity that they often miss the point of why they are doing it. The ESTJ needs to be reminded that often the tasks have a greater meaning and what that meaning is.

Work Environment

The ESTJ is a strong strategic planner and a good manager of people and resources. Their ability to keep track of multiple responsibilities and to follow up on their goals allows them to accomplish a great number of things. They enjoy an environment where the people are organized and outgoing. They prefer rules and policies that are consistent and meaningful.

They are task-oriented and can often miss the personal dynamics of the work setting. Often perceived as blunt, they provide a crisp, impersonal analysis of situations and provide a logical critique of what is going on. Their strength in details and organization gives them a good eye for potential problems and pitfalls in what the group is doing.

They are focused on efficiency and want to accomplish their tasks in the best way, as they define it. They are very good with deadlines and can meet goals on time.

They are very structured in their own work and enjoy operating in a traditional hierarchical system. They like clearly established and understood lines of authority and want to know exactly what their boundaries are. As natural leaders, they are quick to look for opportunities for advancement.

The ESTJ Leader

A natural born leader, the ESTJ combines the outgoing personality of the extrovert with the organizational skills of the judging preference. They are usually adept at working with people and are seen as rational, logical, reliable, and consistent. They prefer the clear authority provided by a hierarchical structure and see themselves as being the top authority for the floor they supervise.

They are able to bring their past experiences to solving problems and as their time on staff grows, they will often rise to positions of authority. If not given opportunities for advancement, the ESTJ RA will often become the RA of the RAs as their natural abilities seek an outlet.

They are quick to take charge, especially in a vacuum and can act with authority that they do not possess if they see the need. For them, it is better to make a bad choice than not to. Others may perceive them to be hard, driven, or even heartless, but their focus is on the ultimate goal, whatever that may be, and if the niceties along the way get bruised, then that is a small price to pay.

Programming

Strong in planning, ESTJs will be able to respond well to deadline requirements and quantifiable programming expectations. They struggle with more vague requirements, such as programming according to needs, unless they are given concrete methods for making those determinations. Once they have some experience under their belt, ESTJs are able to handle uncertain expectations better as they will be able to apply their experience to a new floor of residents and are able to understand how their programming efforts affect the floor community.

Good with people and usually seen as consistent and fair, ESTJs do well with disciplinary concerns, though they can be seen as a bit dictatorial. Designing rules to accomplish the expectations may conflict with the self-governance ideals of many departments because ESTJs take their position as a leader seriously and believe in the authority it conveys. They may set an unrealistic expectation for their residents to follow the established floor hierarchy.

Programs that the ESTJ will likely pursue will be sensible, logical, and things that have a rational order to their system. Physical activities are popular with them, as well programs that can be clearly defined and have demonstrated goals and objectives. With less emphasis on just getting together programs during the first year, they usually focus on trying to actually do something with their residents.

Organization

Like most of the people with the judging preferences, the ESTJ is a natural organizer. They are able to set goals and accomplish what they set out to do. Their sense of accomplishment comes from being able to demonstrate that a task is complete. Whether showing a finished project or simply crossing an item off of their to-do list, the closure that it provides is what drives the ESTJ.

As with their work, their life is one of efficiency and logic. Their personal space and activities reflect it. They are likely to use a planner more efficiently and can probably keep up with more simultaneous activities than others. Their sense of tradition also gives them an inclination to remembering the past. Combining this with their organizational skills, they usually remember or have items from past decisions or discussions which they can access quickly to emphasize their position in a current activity.

Relationship with Residents

ESTJs usually have the ability to establish good rapport with their residents, especially when viewed as the authority presence for the floor. They are able to create good relationships with others when they are perceived as the unbiased third party and will probably work well in dealing with issues of mediation and handling conflict.

As mentioned, the ESTJ will probably struggle with issues of counseling and being the feeling person. They do not develop many deep relationships with the people around them, but they will establish a degree of contact and friendship with most of them. Their ability to be seen as fair goes a long way toward establishing a sense of trust with their residents, but they need to be very aware of their tendency towards bluntness. Their lack of attention to personal issues can result in others perceiving them as mean or unfeeling.

Issues of Concern

ESTJs have areas of concern that they need to be aware of and deal with. Their tendency towards action can often cause them to make rash decisions and they are unwilling to change their mind, even when the circumstances have changed and are no longer valid. This stubbornness can cause them to overlook other possibilities and limit the flexibility that good leaders need when responding to situations.

ESTJs also need to be more aware and concerned about those around them. They can involve others in decision making by asking for and really listening to the advice of others. They need to be more balanced in their feedback. While able to provide criticism easily and quickly, they need to provide compliments for work that they take for granted. If something is supposed to be done right and you do it right, ESTJs do not see the need for praise.

ESTJs need to learn to express their own feelings in a healthier manner. They have the tendency to repress their feelings and not let them out. After repressing their emotions for a long time, they can often erupt over what is seemingly a minor incident; for them however, it was the proverbial straw that broke the camel's back.

Although the ESTJ is a natural leader, this can sometimes cause more harm than good. They can be seen as autocratic and controlling and others may become resentful of their watchfulness. Their desire for efficiency and follow up, when taken to extremes, can become micro-management and a controlling personality. They can be seen as rigid and unyielding in their dealings with others. Their strong sense of right and wrong can lead them to make decisions for others without justification or without the appreciation of others.

Lastly, they need to be aware of their preference towards established way of doing things. This can lead them into a rut where they are basically operating on autopilot. Resistance to change increases over time, especially when they are not challenged in their established routine and habits.

The ISFJ Resident Assistant: The Helping RA

The ISFJ RA is a loyal, sympathetic and considerate staff member who focuses on the practical needs of people. They will go to any lengths to help others, especially if it makes sense to them. They focus on providing practical help and services for the organizations that they are a part of and for the people that they are connected to.

The ISFJ is very comfortable with following rules, especially those that are well defined. Traditions are also important to them as part of the natural and logical ways of maintaining relationships within their groups. Birthdays and other celebrations are a big deal for them; they especially make sure that everyone is remembered.

ISFJs like to know what is expected of them and what the rules of the game are before they start playing. Seeking to please those in authority, whether a parent, teacher, or employer, they will quietly and effectively meet those expectations. However, they do not show a partial grasp of a situation. Instead they prefer to master a skill or ability and to feel comfortable in it before showing others; they avoid being seen as clumsy in their learning process. Security and routine are important to ISFJs and once they have mastered a situation, they will feel safe in their abilities. Change, however, is not something that they will grab onto very willingly.

Like other introverts, ISFJ RAs keep their thoughts and feelings close to themselves. They are likely to have a few close friends that last over the course of their lifetime. ISFJs are generally reluctant to share their problems or concerns with others, or to ask for help when they need it.

Training

ISFJs are good in learning situations because of their desire to please their teachers and their tendency to follow through on their work. They desire to fully know what is expected of them in order to produce the expected results that are required by teachers and trainers. They prefer training to be clear and concise; real work allows them to demonstrate that they have worked hard on their assignments and have actually learned something.

As a sensing type, ISFJ RAs learn best by actually doing. Practical experience allows them to understand and reinforce their learning in context and to master the skills that will be used in their application. With their emphasis on relationships, ISFJs learn best from actual experience.

ISFJs are not good independent study candidates, as they prefer an organized and efficient group to work with in their studies. If they are not able to connect with others who share their sense of organization, they will study alone.

In planning training for the ISFJ, always remember that they need accuracy in the facts presented to them. Provide clear directions on how they are to perform their job. Unlike many types, ISFJs learn very well from a lecture style format as long as it engages their senses. This allows you to use some traditional styles in your presentation as long as you are organized.

Work Environment

The ISFJ RA values a work environment that seeks to provide people with their practical needs. The RA job as a resource person, rule enforcer, counselor, and peer leader is a natural fit for them. Their main difficulty will be in overcoming their own introversion and in becoming more social, though their decisions making based on relationships will provide them with a good sense of balance.

ISFJs are very aware of the routine and details and will go to great lengths to make sure that accuracy is guaranteed. They focus on the specifics and they work hard to make sure that the people they work with agree with that philosophy. Follow through is also very important to them and they work hard to keep up with their duties. They expect the same from their supervisor and coworkers. A supervisor who is disorganized and forgetful will quickly lose respect and authenticity with ISFJs.

As an introvert the ISFJ needs time alone for privacy and quiet in order to be productive. They need calm to focus their efforts and time away to rejuvenate themselves for further efforts. Their desire to provide a practical and helpful service to others allows them to deal with the constant presence of others in the halls, especially those whose behavior does not measure up to their level of commitment. The ISFJ will go to almost any length to help someone in need and will have a poor impression of a fellow staff member who is not as committed.

Order is very important to the ISFJ: things need to be in their proper place in order for them to function and perform. They will organize their world around their values and expect the same of others. While time and structure are very important to them, the needs of those in their care will still come first. Dealing with one of their resident's personal crisis is a priority and will usually override other demands or expectations. They are there for their residents.

The ISFJ Leader

ISFJs are reluctant leaders. They do not actively seek out positions of authority, but rather are asked into them. Because of their sense of duty and obligation they will take on the leadership role intending to do a good job, even though they are not necessarily the best for the job. They focus on what is required by the group or organization, not how the position will benefit them. Their personal focus and organizational strengths provide them with strong tools to be successful in leadership roles. They possess a head for details and will follow the rules and procedures of the system out of their respect for how things are done. They are not the innovators of a group.

Tradition plays a big role for the ISFJ, especially in dealing with others. Respecting lines of authority and hierarchical structure is natural to them and they expect others to do the same. They focus on people and how they function together rather than on completing tasks or projects and they will either defer or ignore outright such tasks if the group's dynamic is faltering and in need of attention.

Normally, the ISFJ prefers to let others take the spotlight. They enjoy working behind the scenes to make sure that what is supposed to be done is done. They care about the needs and values of those around them, especially those in their care.

Programming

Programming is not particularly exciting for the ISFJ though they do it because it is expected of them and is a part of their job. They usually tend towards programs that focus on relationships and the needs and values of their residents. These programs will have to be practical and useful, but they also need to be relevant for the RA to be enthusiastic about them.

Well-organized, ISFJ programmers handle the administrative portions of their job rather well. While not rushing to complete work, they are rarely late with their programming obligations. However, if something came up with a resident that would be their priority.

ISFJs value programming ideas and tools of assessment that are clear, concise, and easy to use. Too much focus on intuitive guesswork or unstructured methods will not interest them. A clear method of identifying issues facing residents, followed by how to address those issues, will greatly increase their motivation.

Organization

Like the rest of the judging types, ISFJs create order in their world. They are conscious of time and commitments, but they do tend to procrastinate. However, they are usually only late for work or appointments when a crisis happens.

ISFJs organize around their values and what is important to them, namely people. They make sure that they have the tools that they need to do their work and that their work allows them to pay attention to the needs of those around them. They are very good at setting detailed goals. In addition, they handle changes and adjust their goals better than other judging types as they view those changes as a part of life.

Relationship with Residents

Because their desire to provide practical help to others is very strong, ISFJs are good with their residents. They seek to help others and will go to extreme lengths for those they see in need. Their solutions may be too practical for some residents as the ISFJ may give the negative side of their personality too much reign in dealing with residents. Telling a resident with an unfaithful significant other to get rid of him or her may be practical advice, but it may not address the real issues the resident is facing.

ISFJs are good about establishing relationships and are usually viewed as a quiet source of support and assistance. They avoid the spotlight and support the primary players. They may not operate as the leader of their community; instead they allow more extroverted personalities to take on those roles. Although it is the ISFJ RA who is really the glue of the group — making sure that things happen as they are supposed to, providing support when needed, and keeping up with the needs of those they are responsible for —they do not feel the need to be actually seen doing the job.

Issues of Concern

Everyone has problems to be dealt with because of their personal preferences, and the ISFJ is no exception. To begin with, the ISFJ tends to be pessimistic about the future and is quick to look on the downside of situations rather than the possibilities for success. Their focus on personal and human experiences can lead them to take a very negative view of the world and what is going to come.

They are not seen as being very tough minded and that impression leads others to think that they cannot handle difficult situations, especially when intense emotional issues are involved. Their desire to help others can paralyze them when no clear solution to the problem is apparent and the person is obviously suffering. For female staff, the ISFJ is one of the least assertive types and has a tendency towards avoiding conflict by turning inward.

Their attraction to history and traditional ways of doing things can lead them to a rut. They can easily fall into the trap of always doing things in the same way if they are not constantly aware of how and why they are doing things. Their organizational skills can also overwhelm them, leading them to plan to excess and over-organize their personal lives and space. Spending too much time planning and preparing allows them to actually avoid dealing with issues or projects that they do not want to face. This can often lead to a degree of inflexibility that strains their relationships with others who wish that they would loosen up.

ISFJs also tend to focus on the present and what is actually occurring in their space. While this is useful in identifying issues that the group may be facing, their practical nature can lead them to focus so heavily on the specifics of a particular situation that they miss the meaning of what those facts are trying to tell them. They can identify the unacceptable behavior of individual residents, but they may not connect those behaviors to deeper issues or as the clues to significant issues that the resident may be dealing with.

The ISFP Resident Assistant: The Caring RA

The ISFP RA is a gentle, compassionate, and open individual. Their flexibility and concern for others are two of their defining traits. They are considerate towards others and are not likely to push their own opinions on another; rather they prefer to persuade others through a subtle and gentle approach, which results in a change in the other person's behavior or beliefs. The ISFP is like the water that slowly wears away the rock just by persistence.

ISFP RAs do not enjoy it when relationships are suffering. They prefer harmony and cooperation among those they work and live with. While they avoid conflict themselves, they act as a mediator and arbitrator when others are in conflict. When friends or co-workers (or residents) are arguing, the ISFP will readily work to help them settle their differences and restore the sense of community that they value.

Care is an apt word for ISFPs as they are drawn to those that need a soft touch or to a person who will provide the same kind of attention that they give. They are at their best when working to promote the welfare of others, and prefer to work behind the scenes to achieve their intended results. The ISFP does not seek the spotlight in what they do; rather their goal is to see the work done well. The values that they hold most dear and personal are the ones that they look for in others, both in their friends and colleagues. Their own values play a strong role in their life: they will often end a relationship if their friends' or colleagues' actions or values result in a real conflict with their own.

Training

As a sensing type, ISFPs do best with practical, hands-on training and learning opportunities. They relate best to what is immediately useful and practical and have difficulty with those topics that are too future oriented or theoretical in nature. They enjoy models and other physical representations of their work as it allows them to directly interact with the item and experience the most sensory excitement from the object.

ISFPs enjoy learning about people. They prefer opportunities that explore the nature of relationships and the human condition and that helps them to understand and figure out a person. However, that knowledge must be readily apparent. While understanding what tools psychology may give them in their job, the theoretical nature of the material results in a struggle for the ISFP.

The need for freedom and flexibility is very prevalent in the ISFP and they have a strong need for that freedom to be able to manifest itself in their learning. They dislike structure and will usually avoid those subjects that are, by nature, too confining for their sense of learning. The ISFP learns in a quiet manner, needing to concentrate to absorb the information that they will later demonstrate through their actions rather than by standard testing methods. ISFPs are not big fans of reading and will usually spend time only on required reading. For them, it's the doing that is worthwhile.

Learning must be relevant in their eyes, though the methodical administrative tasks that the judging types do well at quickly bores them. Because they focus on people, techniques for counseling, peer mentoring, and mediation/arbitration especially appeals to them. Learning practical ways to help their residents resonates with them and captures their attention and focus.

Work Environment

ISFPs need an environment that promotes people working to help others in a practical method as those needs occur. They are not fans of schedules as they feel that people are more important than keeping to an agenda. If someone needs their aid, they are quite willing to sacrifice timeliness or commitments to others, such as meetings or non-people issues. They want to focus on the well-being of others, and are especially aware of those in their responsibility.

ISFPs take a very quiet enjoyment in what they do and they do not seek outward recognition for those efforts. They find benefit in what they accomplish and in helping others. They attend to the practical needs of the people they are responsible for with a degree of flexibility that enables them to quickly adapt their efforts to address those needs.

They need an environment that promotes cooperative efforts in order to achieve their goals. Because it is the condition of the relationships of people that is the critical element in any group or organization's success, relationships between people will always have a higher importance for them than particular tasks. Attend to the needs of the people, and they will be able to attend to the needs of the organization.

As an introvert, ISFP RAs need their private time. A space of their own or the opportunity to work without the distractions of other people or events is a necessary part of their ability to function. While they enjoy their relationships with others, they still need privacy to recharge themselves; however they are still very courteous to others and will often sacrifice their needs to attend to others.

The ISFP Leader

ISFPs are not your typical leaders as they do not seek out such opportunities. They are much more likely to work behind the scenes and support those in leadership positions. They are loyal followers as long as their personal values and those of their leader line up; when those values diverge the ISFP will seek out a new leader. You do not convince an ISFP to change their values; the only way to even try is a slow, non-threatening process of persuasion.

ISFPs seek a cooperative and team-based approach and are not the dynamic, personality-based leaders; rather they are invisible leaders and guide the group to the desired goals with a much more subtle approach. Using personal loyalty to motivate others, they inspire their followers to do what the ISFP feels they need to do. This way they do not command obedience, but rather they get others to do what they are supposed to do naturally.

This way of persuading others allows them to keep to the background while still supporting the efforts of others. This allows them to provide assistance and guide the group, yet maintain their anonymity. This is a skill that they will develop over time, but as RAs they may need some guidance on how to get started.

Programming

ISFP programmers will likely direct their efforts to those programs that either brings in a presenter or those that do not require a visible leader. ISFP RAs do not enjoy being on display so their natural inclination to avoid the spotlight motivates them to design programs where a team or group has responsibility for the success. This can include arts and crafts, food programs where they can feed their people (taking care of a basic need), or simple movies or game nights. They typically shy away from the programs that require them to present information personally.

Team programming is an area they usually enjoy as it allows them to take their preferred place behind the scenes as a hard worker. They do not need to control every aspect of the program as long as everyone involved agrees upon the ultimate goal. If the goal is in conflict, they struggle to put some of their views about caring for the residents' needs forward to the group.

Organization

Like the rest of the perceiving types, ISFPs do not have strong organizational skills. Time and structure are not their priority, nor is completing a particular task. Their enjoyment comes from actually doing something. Whether or not they finish what they start is not a real issue for them, just the fact that they are actively engaged. They can start projects by the dozen, but can they finish them? That is a harder question.

When they do organize themselves, ISFPs organize around their values of flexibility, people, and helping others. They possess the ability to make their environment structured, and they can even follow such a structure if they see how that structure helps those that they care about. Otherwise, they usually prefer to operate on a system that emphasizes freedom from such a structure.

Relationship with Residents

ISFPs have a good relationship with their residents, but it will be on a very quiet and personal level. Their major difficulty will be with residents whose behaviors and values don't live up to theirs, and their natural tendency to avoid those people will conflict with their duties. Developing a community is more difficult for them as their nature directs them to the background and favors a slow, patient approach that rarely works in a residence-hall setting without great effort.

ISFPs excel in counseling and peer support. As an impartial arbitrator and a source of strength, they develop a reputation for caring about their residents that can cause friction when their other duties are lacking. ISFPs can be wonderful RAs in some aspects of the job, but they have to really work hard at the administrative and judicial parts.

Their unwillingness to be mean or hard will often come back to haunt them in confrontations and can be used against them by their residents. They also have difficulty dealing with confrontations as they are not confrontational. They do not enjoy arguments or conflict and usually will go to great lengths to avoid such situations. This can cause them many problems until they learn the consequences of not dealing with those issues directly and immediately. By their second year, ISFPs will probably be better able to deal with conflicts with residents, but they will need a great deal of support to reach that point.

Issues of Concern

Like all of the types, ISFPs struggle with things that make their job difficult. Their inability to deal with confrontations is a major issue as they just don't like being put in that position and will usually go to great lengths to avoid it. Their trusting nature makes them very susceptible to criticism, and pressure from residents, (being seen as the bad guy on the floor) is very difficult for them.

Supervising the ISFP requires not only patience, but also some strong work in getting the RA to talk about their feelings. ISFPs do not talk easily, even though they are feeling things very deeply. Though they are trusting, usually too much so, they are not willing to open up to others and share their true thoughts. Once done, a great deal of self-doubt and criticism is usually discovered.

ISFPs are overly self-critical about what they do. They are hesitant to give themselves credit for the work that they do well, and instead focus on where they are lacking. They can be emotionally hurt rather easily and will usually respond by withdrawing from the individual who wronged them. They may even use such criticism as a proof of their lack of ability. Providing criticism for the ISFP, which will be necessary, is a delicate balancing act that requires tact, patience, and care.

In their quest to help those around them, ISFPs often will not attend to their needs and can suffer as a result. They need to be reminded to take time for themselves and that it is okay to do so. Their introverted nature, combined with a desire to help others, can make them amazing caregivers, but it can also cause them to suffer and not know how to stop. Supervisors need to watch for signs of this and take appropriate actions.

Finally, ISFPs tend to focus so much on the present and what is happening right here and now that they often lose sight of the big picture. Not seeing the context of what their actions may mean outside a particular situation, they can make decisions that may be good for one situation but harmful to others. This is especially true when dealing with people. Their desire to help can cause them to make decisions that may be a short-term solution, but will only aggravate problems later on because they have not been dealt with, only postponed.

The ESFP Resident Assistant: The Social RA

ESFPs are fun-loving and social people who truly enjoy life, especially when they are in situations that focus on relationships and people. They are outgoing personalities who enjoy meeting and interacting with people of various types and ages. Equally good with children, peers, and elders, they easily establish rapport as they naturally accept people without any expectations.

ESFPs are empathetic, generous, and give freely of their time and money for causes and people that they are associated with or identify as their responsibility. They take great pride in bringing people together and building connections and relationships among those they interact with. The ESFP RA is going to be one of the better community builders because of this trait.

ESFPs are very aware of what is going on around them and with the people that they spend time with. Their combined focus on the present moment and on people allows them to be particularly aware of issues that their residents are dealing with, often before the resident is even truly aware of it.

ESFPs are very spontaneous and their natural flexibility allows them to respond well to the unexpected and take advantage of the opportunities that can occur on a floor. Their fun-loving nature is often contagious and can encourage the people they work and live with to make great efforts to enjoy what is happening around them.

As a representative of your department and institution, the ESFP is one of the best RA types. They usually present a very positive and valuable image to others, which results in a very flattering view of the group. They are natural ambassadors for any group, and for a job that is so in line with their personal preferences they shine even better as they usually love their job.

Training

ESFPs, like the rest of the sensing types, prefer practical information to theoretical learning. They have a great ability to remember lots of details and facts, especially ones that reflect on the practical aspects of their job. They prefer that instructions are very clear, and that the steps in any procedure are not only outlined but also free of ambiguity.

ESFPs will respond best to practical demonstrations and activities that allow them to practice new skills before discussing any meaning associated with those skills. In other words, getting them to imagine how a particular situation may arise and how they may respond will be difficult until they are placed in that situation. They will usually respond very well to training activities such as Incident Street or Behind Closed Doors.

As an extrovert, ESFPs learn best when they are able to interact and learn with others, rather than individually. They learn best in groups where they can discuss, share, and draw on the group's thoughts and experiences to discover answers. Reading or working by themselves is difficult as they will often lose interest or become easily distracted by more interesting things.

Lastly, ESFPs need to feel some kind of personal connection with the teacher or presenter if they are going to trust that person and the material that they are trying to teach. Although the methods and ways that the presenter uses is not as important to them, they prefer a more interactive approach to show that the person cares about them personally. To show appreciation for that caring teacher, they will make great efforts to learn and demonstrate understanding.

Work Environment

ESFPs prefer to be in surroundings that are as exciting and dynamic as they are. They operate best in an environment that is focused on people and relationships and one that deals with the realities of the present. They are willing to work on tasks and recognize the importance of doing work. However, to be able to focus on those tasks the relationships between the people involved must be working well or they will divert their energy to addressing those relationships.

Aware of their surroundings, ESFPs enjoy working in a place that is attractive and pleasing to the eye. This preference, if encouraged, can translate into great visual work by the RA in the forms of signs, banners, and other personal touches that add to the atmosphere of their floor and building. Encouraging their contributions and suggestions will work wonders on their motivation levels, as they are able to personally make their area look better.

As a feeling type, ESFPs need harmony at work. This includes the connections between residents, fellow staff, and supervisory personnel. A hall, area, or department with too much conflict will distress them and hinder their ability to function at their best. Their desire to work with others draws them to occupations and jobs that allow for high levels of interactions. The RA job is very good for them as it focuses on people and deals with the relationships that they can develop with residents.

The ESFP Leader

The ESFP leader operates best when encouraging participatory contributions from all of the people involved. They focus on the positive relationships of the team and create a sense of camaraderie among the staff or residents. When all the different types of people are able to work and play together without conflicts or issues, they feel successful.

As this is rarely the case with any group, ESFPs often function as peacemaker or mediator and can bring opposing sides together to some kind of accord. They promote the social aspects of the group and work very hard to bring people, often with very different ideas and goals, together for the group's overall purpose.

With their attention to the present, they are very good at responding to most kinds of crisis that can arise in the halls. They can deal with just what is happening before them and focus on the needs of the moment. This focus allows them to deal with the immediacy of an issue without concern for what is yet to come. However, this can cause problems if set procedures and policies are not clearly explained to them. They are able to follow a plan very well, but if left to their own initiative, they will pay more attention to the present than to any future implications of their actions.

Lastly, ESFPs leaders actively seek input and participation from others. They want everyone to take a role in what is happening, which means that they should be able to contribute freely, and will expect the same from their supervisor and team. Dealing with a more autocratic style will be very difficult for them and can lead to conflict with that authority. For their community, they will likely have a very involved floor with many residents contributing to the creation of their programs, activities, and the relationships among the residents.

Programming

ESFPs do very well in programs that deal with the people on their floor. Programs that promote connections and coming together hold a very special place for them, and they will direct most of those efforts to meeting the needs of their residents. If tuned into the residents, as they usually are, ESFPs will be successful in their efforts because they have taken the time to know and understand their residents.

Spontaneous programs are something that they enjoy as it gives free rein to their flexible nature. Having the ability to respond to the needs of the moment without a great deal of planning and preparation allows them to live in the moment, a place that they enjoy most.

ESFPs will most likely struggle with the advance planning requirements unless they feel that the floor's community is established and functioning well. In that case, they are able to handle the responsibilities of prior planning and can better attend to administrative duties. However, this means that at the beginning of a year, when the residents and the community are in its formative stage, ESFPs will spend their energy on making the connections between the residents rather than following a plan that does not address the immediate needs of their residents.

Organization

As a perceiving type, ESFPs usually struggle with issues of time management, organization, and follow through associated with the RA position. They are more focused on doing the job than following an agenda or path set by someone not intimately connected with what they are doing on their floor. Tasks that are presently useful to them will be organized and done well; otherwise they will often be discarded. This can include theories of behavior and other long term planning that they cannot identify with until they have had the personal experience of doing the job. As ESFPs gain experience, they begin to appreciate and use those tools that the more future-oriented types naturally accept.

Their sense of organization focuses on being practical and dealing with the relationships of people. Procedures that may be difficult for them to understand (logs, reports, etc.) can be explained in terms of how they affect the harmony of the group and help the supervisor to understand what is going on. Explained in terms that the ESFP values, they are more likely to accept those requirements and help encourage others to do so as well.

Relationship with Residents

ESFP RAs will develop good relationships with their residents as they are so focused on people. Making sure that roommates get along, that people are respecting each other, and that common space is being used for the benefit of all are areas in which they excel. They believe that harmony is good for the overall atmosphere of a community and will work to make the hall a better place to live for all of those involved.

One issue that ESFPs need to work on is their natural tendency to accept others as they are. This means that often they will either not recognize problem behaviors among their residents, or will see them as part of an individual's personality that is not open for discussion. While great for dealing with people one-on-one, this tendency may cause them to ignore or excuse those behaviors that others in the community are not so willing to forgive or overlook.

As a general rule, ESFPs know best what is going on with their residents. Their attention to people and their focus on what is currently happening allow them to be very perceptive of how others are feeling and what problems they are faced with. This ability often means that the ESFP RA can detect problems between residents before they become too large or too difficult to address. The main issue is getting the RA to step in at that point and help resolve the conflict rather than wait for it to rise to a more difficult level.

Issues of Concern

As with all the types, ESFPs have issues that they need to be aware of and address. First, they focus a great deal of their time and energy on relationships. This can lead to a tendency to over socialize so that other tasks or responsibilities are pretty much ignored. By trying to be the friend and social director for their floor, they can lose sight of the job and get into trouble with their supervisor for not doing their other responsibilities.

They also need to be aware of their tendency to get excited about the new things that come up that they ignore what they are currently doing. Projects that take time to plan and develop can get started with enthusiasm but the ESFP can lose that enthusiasm and not finish the projects that they start. Their supervisor needs to help them develop follow-through skills that will allow them to finish what they start. Remember, it's not that they don't want to do something, rather it either takes them too long to finish or other things catch their eye and draw their attention and energy away.

Dealing with priorities is another area that the ESFP always struggles with. Having to choose between responsibilities will often boil down to what is the most immediate crisis or which affects the most people or the relationships of the group. Having to choose tasks, especially ones that do not rank high in the two categories above, is very difficult for them even when they recognize the importance of those tasks to others.

Lastly, ESFPs need to look before they leap. Their focus on the moment can often lead to trouble when they dash forward to solve a problem or start a project without taking the time necessary to think it through and plan ahead. ESFPs do not actively consider the ramifications of their actions, so their supervisor will need to help them develop their awareness of this issue.

The ESFJ Resident Assistant: The Assessing RA

ESFJ RAs are helpful staff members who value people, personal values, traditions, and getting the job done. They work well with others, especially on teams or group projects. They like to see things done and completed, especially those activities or projects that provide help or support for others. Very community-minded, the ESFJ is a dedicated and often tireless worker in helping others.

ESFJs are very responsible and reliable for doing the things that they commit to in a job. If they say that they will do something, or even think that they will, it usually means that they will no matter what. Clear expectations help them to do what others expect or need them to do. They are very cooperative and willing to share responsibilities and duties with those around them.

ESFJs are very traditional and their beliefs reflect this. They believe that if they tell the truth and work hard, then they will be rewarded and recognized. When it doesn't happen, they feel violated and turned upon, which means that they can lose their trust in authority. Concepts such as floor charges or group responsibility are very contrary to their mindset and beliefs.

ESFJs have a very strong sense of civic responsibility and they view their roles very seriously. They see jobs that help others as not only important but truly critical, and they will give it their all. As an RA, they will spend a great deal of time and energy toward being the best RA for their residents, according to their interpretations of the residents' needs.

Training

ESFJs prefer to learn in a social setting that have very clear expectations and organization. They like to know their schedule and what the final product or outcome will be. Being able to plan, study, or prepare in advance gives them security and makes them more likely to take a strong interest in the material.

Like the other sensing types, ESFJs want the material to be practical and useful rather than theoretical in nature. They enjoy hands-on experiences that allow to them to really know what is being discussed. They prefer clear, laid-out procedures for handling things that are expected by their supervisors and do not need a lot of flexibility or freedom in how things are accomplished.

ESFJs prefer their learning to deal with real life people and their problems. They will retain and understand information better if it demonstrates applicability to real life and people. Examples of how training methods have paid off or how previous staff members have used the information to benefit others will have the maximum impact on the ESFJ.

ESFJs are talkers. They want to discuss what is going on and training is no exception. Discussion groups, question and answers, and other opportunities for them to verbalize their thoughts and hear the thoughts of others will charge them up. They need to socialize and feel out others in order to help them see the value of what is being presented.

Lastly, they learn best in situations where there is a personal connection or relationship with the presenter. Their need to identify with that person means that if they do not like or trust the person, or if they have not had the opportunity to see the presenter in a human light, then they will be slow to listen or trust the information provided. Enough participation and practical needs addressed in a presentation will help, but time spent establishing a relationship will greatly improve their learning.

Work Environment

ESFJs enjoy working in an atmosphere full of people dedicated to helping others and cooperating with each other. They have a strong need for harmony in their relationships and between the people around them. Working with a people focus and the goal of helping others, the RA position is one that will naturally draw the ESFJ personality to the job.

Cooperation is very important to them and they are very good at getting people to work together. Often a peacemaker of any group, they are quick to try and get people to resolve conflicts. Their need to make everyone happy and get along can cause them to forgo other tasks in favor of dealing with the people issues.

ESFJs look for places that are warm and friendly and this often shows up on their floor. If encouraged, they will put great effort into decorating their floor and their room as a place for others to feel welcome and comfortable. Their organizational skills also allow them to make that welcoming place look neat and orderly without developing the coldness that can often be associated with structure and organization.

ESFJs need to be given clear job expectations. Plain talk is necessary for them to see what their supervisor wants. It also allows them to schedule and plan how they will achieve those expectations. When priorities or policies change, ESFJs have difficulty dealing with it and will need special attention. Putting changes in terms of human needs, as well as much advance notice as possible, will greatly assist them in accepting those changes.

The ESFJ worker respects rules and authority well as long as the reason for the way things are done is based on helping others. Rules or policies that do not have a human element, or the human element is not explained well, cause them difficulty and distress.

Lastly, ESFJs have a tough time with criticism even if it is designed to help them. Their need for approval is very strong and anything less than praise causes them to be mentally distressed. While they may even agree with such feedback, until they make the corrections and have that improvement recognized by their supervisor, they will not be in a good place. So when giving the ESFJ constructive feedback, be sure and follow up when they correct the behavior and are now meeting expectations.

The ESFJ Leader

ESFJ leaders lead through the relationships that they establish with the people around them. Using a very personal and close style, they lead by paying attention to the needs and wants of the people around them and they are usually in tune with the group's situations and needs. Expertise in a particular area is not as important for them as being able to get along well with everyone.

ESFJs are very good about keeping others informed. Their desire to communicate creates a strong two-way flow of information between them and the people around them and this atmosphere of active participation will usually generate good results.

ESFJs are very dedicated, service-oriented people and their high levels of expectations often lead them to expect the same level and degree of commitment from those around them. They will try to help fellow staff who do not put in the same amount of effort. However, once a problem is resolved, then the failure is quickly forgiven and the ESFJ moves on.

Because of their desire to keep harmony among their group they may ignore performance issues because they believe that addressing them would damage their relationships. Just as they struggle with feedback, they struggle to provide criticism even when it is necessary for the other person's development and growth.

Programming

Their ability to know what is going on with their residents, their attention to people's needs and wants, and their desire for planning and organization all come together to create a programmer who knows what residents need and want (assessment), who plans (intentional programming) out activities, and who follows up on the associated administrative tasks. They are definitely one of the best programming types when it comes to meeting most departmental goals associated with this aspect of the RA job.

They are also very good at recognizing programs that will be popular with their residents and are likely to have good participation. They are not as skilled at spontaneous programs as they prefer to plan out and follow their schedule, so making changes will be difficult for them. A clear expectation of the kind and quantity of programs is very important, though they are likely to do more than required if they see their programs as ways of getting people connected and building friendships.

Organization

Like most of the judging types, ESFJs have good organizational skills. They like to organize their environment so that they have access to the tools and information that they need to help others. They will focus most of their efforts around people and relationship issues as it allows them to keep things structured and people-centered.

Their strong ties and interest in people is a central factor in their life and it shows in their organizational skills. They are very conscious of time, especially keeping appointments with other people. They also are very good at remembering a large number of details about people so that they can be viewed as not only interested, but also as someone who cares about the people around them.

Relationship with Residents

A social person, ESFJs will usually establish a very good relationship with their residents due to their willingness to accept others as they are. Though they may have some ideas about what is best for other people, they always try to keep the peace and ensure that everyone gets along. ESFJs do very well in keeping up with what is going on with all of their residents, and are aware of potential problems that may occur.

Their reticence about providing negative or constructive feedback make it difficult for them to handle disciplinary and judicial issues. They do not like to do anything that hurts the relations among their people; this may lead them to ignore problems or situations where someone can express anger or hurt towards them for doing their job.

This tendency can also show up even though the RA is willing to be the peacemaker and help people resolve conflicts because they may not be able or willing to look beyond the surface for signs of something greater or more serious. This can cause them to deal only with the symptoms of a conflict, which is often not the true cause of the dispute. It can also let them believe that if people are not fighting or arguing, then all is well.

Issues of Concern

Like all types, ESFJs take their strengths so far that they become detrimental to their best level of performance. While being very social and truly enjoying life, they have a tendency to avoid facets of their life that are not as emotionally rewarding. This means that they can neglect academics and the administrative responsibilities in order to pay more attention to the parts that they like. To help counter this tendency, they need assistance in seeing those parts as necessary to continue the social aspects of being an RA.

ESFJs like harmony among the people around them. It will take time and experience before they truly begin to see the value and worth of and letting conflict occur. Just hiding a problem does not mean that it is dealt with, but that is what they will often believe. They need to be taught how managed conflict can be helpful for all parties, especially when deeper issues are involved than what is currently being discussed (e.g., fights over phone messages).

Another area that they need to work on for their own development is learning moderation and how to say no. Their desire to please everyone will lead them into taking on more responsibilities than they can truly handle. Burn-out and stress are common as they try and be all things to all people. Learning that saying no means getting others to learn to be independent is a critical hurdle for their thought process.

Be aware of their tendency to narrow their focus too much on the here and now. Unable to see the ramifications of their actions leads them into trouble, especially when they feel that they know best and are acting for someone's best interest. This can also manifest as the tendency to get stuck in a habit or a rut. Because they are not able to see other possible ways or better alternatives, they can ignore new ways or opportunities for change in their determination to stick to what they know.

Lastly, ESFJs need to recognize the different priorities and levels of importance that others place on what they do. Service and work for people is so important to them that they usually give all they have, and more, to provide for others. Not everyone is going to place that kind of emphasis or importance on the relationship aspect of the RA job. Accepting that their co-workers will contribute differently does not mean that they contribute less. While ESFJs are willing to accept others as they are, they can be less forgiving when they feel that others are not giving them the attention that they deserve.

The INFJ Resident Assistant: The Idealistic RA

The INFJ is a future-oriented person who seeks to not only understand him/herself but also the rest of humanity. INFJs have a strong compassion for other people and look toward creating and maintaining harmony in the relationships around them. They enjoy their interactions with other people, but their introverted nature tends toward smaller gatherings and fewer, closer associates. Not one for big events or parties, they tend to be more isolated and solitary in nature.

INFJs are artistic and creative and enjoy activities that allow their creativity to manifest in their work. To draw their interest, these projects should have opportunities for independent work that allows them to either work on their own or in a small, close-knit group. They especially like projects that allow them to demonstrate their appreciation for the work or efforts of others (e.g., photo albums, memory books, and recognition and award activities).

While quiet in nature, they have a fierce devotion to their ideals and values and will hold on to them over loyalty to a person or an organization. Their ideals are very important to them and they willingly give their time and energy to their cause. They are focused on a person-centered ideal that promotes the value of the individual and recognizes the work, efforts, or accomplishments of people. The potential and possibilities of people are of major concern for them.

Complex thinkers, they are able to deal with abstract and difficult issues, but usually in their own time and their own way. They need to process their thoughts internally but they can follow patterns well and can see how actions and consequences can connect, especially where people are concerned.

The INFJ is usually a compassionate and caring individual who enjoys being a helper and provider to others. Giving of themselves is natural for INFJs, and they enjoy being able to affect others in a positive manner. They are great observers of the people around them and are usually in tune with what people are dealing with, especially those they are connected to or responsible for.

Training

INFJ RAs are welcome in any instructional setting as they combine a natural inquisitiveness and desire to understand with a desire to personally please their instructors. They have a strong need for instructors to arouse their desire to learn and provide them with personal attention. They enjoy establishing personal relationships with the instructor and use that connection to further their own learning.

INFJs like material to be presented in such a way that their meaning and underlying roots are explained to them. They prefer to understand the why's rather than the what's. Their intuitive preference means that they are not so concerned about facts or details, but rather they focus on the meaning, patterns, and ideas that the material represents. Their intuitive nature allows them to see the value in developmental theories and models.

INFJs are good readers and prefer to learn alone, which allow them to digest the material and consider it before sharing their thoughts and responding to the material. They will usually not demonstrate full comprehension of the material right away, but will demonstrate it later in the educational process. They prefer to express their ideas and thoughts in writing and will respond to formal testing about training material fairly well. Being able to reflect and expand on their thoughts quietly will allow them to present their understanding in the best light.

INFJs, while being focused on relationships and how they interact with others, have little difficulty challenging authority when the information or material does not measure up to their understanding or experience. They are very concerned with both clarity and making sure that goals are defined and understood. Contradictions in policies and/or procedures results in confusion and difficulty in the learning process. They must resolve any conflicts, real or otherwise, in their own minds before they can continue listening and learning from instructors. Presenters need to make sure that their questions or concerns are addressed or the INFJs will not get the maximum benefit from a training session.

Work Environment

INFJs are drawn into jobs where they feel their actions and time will make a difference to people. Their ideals also play a strong role in their decision making about what kinds of work they are willing to do. They can quickly become zealous promoters of the RA job and role if it is marketed correctly and if they see the potential for helping others (usually by seeing a person's potential made real by a devoted staff member).

INFJs need, in addition to feeling that their job is worthwhile to others, to feel respected. They strongly need to see and feel that certain values, such as honesty and integrity, are not only upheld but are core to their mission. If they lose respect for the values of their supervisor, they will quickly lose their passion for the job. To truly succeed at any job, INFJs need to make sure that they have the time and opportunity for quiet, individual work and reflection. Without this chance to consider the possibilities and their options, INFJs become off-centered and can quickly lose their effectiveness.

INFJs are very good organizers of tasks and skills. Their understanding of people gives them the skill to match the abilities of the people to the needs of the tasks, resulting in a good balance of resources. They enjoy working in a job where harmony is strong and have difficulties dealing with conflict or unhappiness that they cannot address. They are good at following up on their commitments and responsibilities.

INFJs are hard workers and want to make sure that their work is actually done before they move on or stop to enjoy their successes. They want to be able to use their strong set of values in the job and see how their ideas and efforts affect the lives of others. They do not enjoy the typical wrangling between personalities as people struggle for dominance and promote personal agendas, and they resent when honesty and hard work are not given the appreciation that they deserve.

The ISFJ Leader

INFJs lead with a vision of what they think is in the best interests of the overall group. This can be both a good thing and a bad thing in the RA role. In the beginning stages of the community, they are able to plan and implement ideas designed to fit their vision of what the residents or the other staff members need fairly easily. The difficulty comes when others demand a bigger role in determining what the group needs. INFJs can have difficulty letting others make decisions that do not meet their own personal vision of the needs of the group.

INFJs seek to win cooperation from their group instead of forcing or compelling obedience. This is a result of their desire to have good personal connections and an acute awareness of how their actions can affect others. The INFJ is an intentional leader; he/she actively seeks to take on such roles. Because of their organizational skills and ability to see possibilities, they usually have a good idea of what they are going to do as well as what they believe those actions will result in among their students.

The INFJ leader has long-term goals and not only the vision of what is to come, but usually a good plan on how to get there. They may, however, overlook some of the practical aspects and requirements of achieving those goals. They are quiet leaders and will seek to inspire others through their actions and commitment to those goals. They are not spotlight seekers, but prefer to have their accomplishments speak for what they believe and are capable of doing. INFJs sometimes do not receive the praise they deserve for their actions due to their reserved nature.

Programming

With an emphasis on their relationships with residents and how their actions, and the actions of others, can affect people, INFJs will usually host programs designed to promote interactions that can be controlled and planned out. Spontaneous ideas and programs that can easily get out of control are not in their comfort zone and they will probably shy away from them. With their more reserved nature, they prefer others to do the on-stage work of the program. This can be an increase in presenters, more co-sponsorships with other staff who will be the star, programs where there is more opportunity for personal attention to attendees, or greater control in the flow and development of the program itself.

INFJ RAs have to be aware of all the procedures and steps in doing their programs, as details are never their strong suit. Their organizational skills will provide them with a great deal of security, especially if they have a checklist or guide to the various stages of their programs. A general list of what needs to be done for a program (e.g., get approval, turn in a form, ask for money, etc.) will give them a much better chance of not missing an important but, to them, an uninteresting step in the process.

INFJs will probably never be the big showmen that some of the other types can be, and will not gravitate toward programs that have much of the dynamic energy that the extroverted types can produce. But in group programs or co-programs, they can provide amazing support and work very hard towards making sure that the program succeeds. They can usually increase overall attendance to programs by calling in on the positive credit that they have established with their residents.

Organization

Like the other judging types, the INFJ is good at organizational tasks, works with a plan, and proceeds toward completing that plan. Lists, planners, and other tools will be natural for them, although they are more likely to organize their space and time by internal concerns and ideas. Although external concerns and issues impact and affect them, it will not be the determining factor.

They are good with time concerns and are rarely tardy but they struggle with changes to the established plan or schedule. INFJs are usually able to juggle multiple tasks and concerns, but usually weigh those that affect people directly as being more important.

Relationship with Residents

INFJs establish relations with their residents on a one-to-one basis, which allows them the opportunity for more personal contact in a smaller setting. Not one for small talk, they usually establish good relations with residents due to their genuine interest in others, as long as they are able to control the development of the relationship. Being in a highly-visible position will be a struggle for them if they cannot find ways to recharge their personal batteries with private or small activities. They will usually grow comfortable interacting with their residents as the relationship develops over the course of the year. Once they have a personal connection with each resident, then dealing with them in a group setting is no longer an issue or concern.

INFJs have a strongly optimistic view of what residents are capable of and what they can do, and this belief will usually communicate itself to the residents so that they know that their RA believes in them. This ability usually allows the RA to overcome his/her quiet nature and establish healthy bonds with the residents. Residents will often view the RA as quiet and reserved, but dependable and interesting.

Issues of Concern

Like all types, INFJs have some issues that will impact their job performance. Communication can be an issue, as with all of the introverted types, as they may not express any of their held beliefs or expectations regarding the responsibilities or duties of others. Their unhappiness with another person's failure to live up to their measure can manifest as personal conflict, dislike, or they may distance themselves from that person. This can show up in their relations with residents, fellow staff, or supervisors. They also have rather high, and sometimes unrealistic, expectations of themselves, which result in a great deal of stress and unhappiness with the job when they feel that they are not living up to their potential.

INFJs can also be stubborn and can ignore evidence, facts, or data that does not match up to their beliefs or values. They can be somewhat closed-minded and partial with their residents. If they have established a persona or standard of behavior for a particular resident, they may go to great lengths to maintain that image even in the face of contradictory evidence (e.g., even thought the facts suggest that a perceived trouble maker is innocent, the INFJ may still believe he/she is guilty).

INFJs are unwilling to criticize or provide feedback to others. This prevents them from being honest about issues that they have or from dealing with their concerns in a healthy manner. This often leads them to hold in their thoughts until they reach the boiling point and just erupt much to the confusion and surprise of those around them. This reticence can also make it hard for them to stand up for themselves. It is often difficult for them to get noticed or taken seriously as leaders, or even as capable people, and their ideas and thoughts will not get the attention that they deserve.

The INFJ can also struggle with following the path or instructions of others. They are independent and prefer to do things their own way. In a position where uniformity and standard procedures are the norm, they will need to understand why it is important and be provided with ways in which they can put their mark on how they do things without sacrificing the departmental needs in the process.

The INFP Resident Assistant: The Perfectionist RA

INFPs are very deeply involved in their beliefs and in what they do. Quiet but warm individuals, they are caring and take a genuine interest in those around them, especially those for whom they feel responsible. Their quiet reflection gives them the ability to often see the true motivations and meanings behind the words and behaviors of those around them. This insight gives them the ability to establish some very good relationships, which often comes as a large surprise to those who tend to overlook and forget them.

Their need for privacy and independence means that they can be difficult to know and they often struggle a great deal before taking on leadership roles. When they do, they tend to gravitate towards those roles that are different from the norm. RA positions with special responsibilities or unique programming/population issues are attractive to them, especially if they have the freedom to exercise their personal creativity.

The INFP RA struggles to ask for help and assistance. At first glance they seem to take on too much to finish, but they will usually come through on their commitments even if it is by the skin of their teeth. They also hate to be seen as either needing others or as being wrong. This combination can lead them to make assumptions based on their own beliefs and values rather than simply asking for clarification. They dislike to show their ignorance by asking for help, especially in a group setting.

INFPs usually find relaxation or fun in solitary pursuits like reading or writing. These allows them to reflect on what they are experiencing and gives them time to see how everything is fitting into their value system. They are extremely determined when dealing with something that's important to them and will not give up. If they strongly believe in something, expect it to stay in the forefront of their thoughts.

Training

INFPs are very able students and enjoy complex and new material, especially those that deal with the why's and how's of things. They do not focus on details and material that does not have a personal hook for them is quickly put aside for other interests. Their ability to master difficult material is very good, but only when they have some vested interest in what they are studying.

Reading and writing are very important to INFPs, as is artistic expression. They enjoy being able to apply their creativity and can have difficulty following established patterns and rote ways of doing things. They best express their understanding in written form and do well in testing situations. They need quiet for serious work and while they enjoy working with other students, they limit those opportunities to a relatively small percentage of their total work.

INFPs enjoy flexibility in their learning, as their pleasure in being able to show their own way of interpreting material is very high. Standard or cookie-cutter ways of doing things are definite de-motivators and can cause them to disconnect from the entire process. Instructors need to be personal and inspire enthusiasm for the material, and allow the INFP to develop a personal relationship with them. A personal connection helps INFPs focus on the material and enjoy the experience, a definite requirement for them to get the most out of the presentation.

Deadlines and other time issues are difficult for the INFP, but very necessary. Their perfectionist streak can cause them to not want to turn in assignments or finish projects because they could always be made better. Strict controls on time help the INFP to focus and commit to finishing projects.

Work Environment

The INFP RA likes to work in a friendly environment with people who share a common purpose. Their value-driven motivation can result in conflicts with other staff members who may see it is as just a job and not a major priority. They like cooperation in the activities of their work and do not like dealing with the bureaucratic aspect of jobs. They dislike rules and regulations and often ignore them in favor of their own way of doing things.

Work should be both fun and meaningful for them, which makes the RA job a good fit if the administrative tasks involved are not too onerous. The INFP is very persuasive and is able to bring people together for a common goal or purpose. Their ability to lead through a more subtle method means that they do not often get recognized for their work. INFPs enjoy being recognized for what they do, but they rarely like the spotlight. They prefer recognition by the supervisor in a one-on-one situation or other similar methods that allow them to know that their efforts are noticed without it being emphasized to the group.

Difficulties with others are mostly likely to occur when the values of staff are different or if there is some conflict present between other group members. The INFP does not like the presence of conflict and will withdraw in the hope that it will resolve itself. INFPs do not enjoy confrontations and will usually keep themselves as far from them as possible.

The INFP Leader

INFP leaders are subtle leaders compared to the other types. Their approach facilitates the involvement of others rather than directing the group. A very inclusive leader, the INFP will work to make sure that everyone feels a part of the group and will use praise and other methods of appreciation to encourage positive behavior from the group. However, the INFP will struggle with providing criticism to others, even if it is presented in a constructive manner.

A very persistent personality, the INFP continues to work to achieve success. They like to work independently and may have trouble sharing issues or concerns with the rest of the group. Their private nature only reinforces this. As a leader, their preference for independence is also evident in that they give others their independence, even if that is not necessarily the best for that person.

INFPs do not like conflicts as they are not an aggressive personality type. This can cause them to ignore or trivialize real problems that threatens the effectiveness of their group and can paralyze the functioning of that group. They have a tendency to want to just do everything themselves to make sure that it is done right, and when conflicts paralyze the group it only reinforces this belief.

Programming

INFPs will usually be able to come up with rather interesting and different programs, thanks to their independent and creative tendencies. Their desire to do things their own way encourages them to try and do their job so as to distinguish themselves from others. Their personal values and belief systems also play a role in determining the kinds of programs that they will promote. For example, if women's issues are a big concern for the INFP RA, then she will direct a great deal of her energy towards that subject, even if her residents are not as committed to it.

The administrative side of the programming requirements, especially timeline, will be an area that the INFP struggles with. If you have specific dates for programs, the INFP will need to be firmly reminded about them on a regular basis. Paperwork will also not be a priority for them as it is just a detail in the much bigger picture of their planning.

INFPs will usually enjoy spontaneous programs that personally involve their residents and can be counted on to take advantage of fortuitous situations. Reserved in nature, the INFP RA will not seek the spotlight or try to control the presentation of the program, but will put in a great deal of energy to make sure it succeeds. However, they may forget the cups for the drinks while still managing to present a wonderful program.

Organization

INFPs struggle with organization and time issues. While they have a sense of what is important and can often meet those requirements, they need a strong and firm authority holding them to deadlines. INFPs have a tendency to start many projects and will move on to something new before finishing existing efforts. Although they do not lose interest, the immediacy lessens when other projects draw their attention. In addition, because of their perfectionism they feel that a project is not really ready yet, so they want to continue to work on it. If given the opportunity, the INFP can delay finishing something indefinitely.

In performing jobs or tasks, the INFP does not follow any particular pattern or sense of logic. Often whim or other extraneous factors will cause them to do things in an apparently random manner. This is their creativity and independence manifesting as they resist following someone else's plan.

INFPs are sentimental and will often keep everything that has any personal value, making them appear as major pack rats. The advantage is that despite holding onto things, they have a sense of propriety and will often hide their collections rather well so it may not appear that they are keeping things.

Finally, remember that for the INFP RA, doing a task is not exciting. They appear to be very absent-minded, especially about details, but the reality is that often this carelessness will result in their discovery of new ways of doing things that are often better or easier for others to follow. Practicality is just not important to them as it is to many of the other types, so they struggle when trying to meet someone else's requirements.

Relationship with Residents

INFP RAs can establish good personal relationships with their residents, though it may take them a while to do so. Intuitive and able to see beyond the surface, INFPs are often able to detect problems and issues facing residents that are not readily apparent to others. This connection with their residents will allow them to be rather effective in counseling and advising. However, they need to be aware of their own prejudices and beliefs and should avoid trying to change their residents if they want to continue being valuable to them.

Confronting inappropriate behavior by residents is going to be an area of difficulty for the INFP. Their combined natural tendency to avoid conflict and their belief that a problem will work out if left alone prevents them from taking direct action to prevent escalation. While they struggle with the judicial aspect of the job, the INFP RA can learn about the consequences of failing to act. Their supervisor needs to help them see those potential consequences as well as to accept the judgment of others, which will probably take some effort. The INFP, if they last until the second year, will probably be one of those staff members that has to learn their lesson about being proactive.

Their good and kind sense of humor allows them to be seen as approachable and entertaining and if, they will trust in their training and their abilities, can easily be as successful with their residents as the more extroverted types. Knowing that they tend to be private and reserved, INFP RAs need to take special efforts to reach out to their residents and let others inside their barriers. This will make their residents feel comfortable with them, as well as identify them as the authority for the community.

Issues of Concern

We have already touched on some of the issues concerning the role of the INFP RA. The biggest is probably their hesitancy to confront conflicts and aggression directly. This causes them to underplay roommate conflicts, behavioral issues, and other disruptions to their community. If they are encouraged to use the relationships that they establish with residents to resolve these issues, they can usually be effective. Getting them out of the mindset that things will resolve themselves is a major step.

INFPs also need to learn how to deal with their of perfectionism. This can often cause them to undervalue their own efforts despite having done an acceptable or even a very good job. This feeling of inadequacy can cripple their ability and growth unless they see that their work was good and that it was noticed. This is where the observant supervisor will be able to help the RAs look at their work in an objective manner.

Their idealistic nature causes them to ignore the real facts and details of their environment if those facts do not fit into their vision or ideal. Learning to accept reality and adjust their plans and views to the facts of a situation will help them to be more successful. This can also prevent them from giving fair value to the ideas of others that do not hold with their own. Because they have "the one way," they struggle to accept the views of others.

Supervisors can help the INFP learn to say no. INFPs tend to take on a great deal of projects and tasks and though they often manage to pull it off, it does take its toll on the wellness of the person. Reducing commitments allows them to spend more energy on what is important to them and to better view their own efforts as positive.

Creating action plans that allow the INFP to be creative, independent, and realistic is also important. While they need to feel control over what they are doing, they also need to operate with the rest of the group. This may mean paying more attention to administrative responsibilities, departmental rules, and standardized ways of doing things. By creating a system for them which ensures that all the necessary steps are taken, INFPs can focus their energies on what is important to them without causing problems with their supervisor.

The ENFP Resident Assistant:
The Adventurous RA

The ENFP RA is a very enthusiastic person with strongly-developed social skills. Able to connect with many different kinds of people, they are undeniably a people-person. Their interests, values, and decisions all are based on the values and interests that they have in the people around them. Their natural sense of exuberance and excitement is very contagious to those around them. They are always in the middle of some activity and they usually manage to bring lots of other people along for the ride.

Possessing a very changeable personality, the ENFP RA seems to be, and is usually, into everything. Anything that interests them will gather their attention and they can apply a great deal of energy pursuing that interest. Reading exhaustively about a topic and talking to everyone they can find, ENFPs try to learn everything that they can about anything that catches their attention. However, when its time to actually use this knowledge, the ENFP is usually onto something new and more interesting.

ENFPs are very good about seeing and noticing what other people around them are doing and are capable of doing. They appreciate the efforts of others and are usually very quick to demonstrate their appreciation. They also have a very good sense of the potential of the people around them. As an RA, this translates into a good ability to get residents involved and doing new things. The ENFP is a firm believer in people. This respect and trust shows through in their interactions with others and is a powerful source of motivation for the people around them.

The ENFP is usually a gifted speaker, especially in social or personal settings. Able to communicate well and express their ideas clearly, ENFPs are quick to offer their thoughts and ideas with the group. They most enjoy the beginning of any project or venture and their energy for the project will spread to others very quickly. The difficulty lies when the ENFP has the responsibility for the project's completion. Their love of beginnings and new things often results in their moving on to new things before finishing their responsibilities.

Training

The ENFP is a curious student who prefers variety in their learning, both in the material presented and in the methods used to present it. Highly-structured plans or training that only allows for one style of learning quickly turn them off as they are unable to focus on the material. They need different learning methods (lectures, activities, group discussions, etc.) to keep them stimulated.

New ideas and possibilities are fascinating to the ENFP, especially if it relates to people. Training about student development, establishing community, and personal relationships attract their attention as well as any material dealing with people. Their main difficulty comes in learning all of the details and facts of administration. Their attention is not directed towards the facts of work, but the goal and aspirations. Their sense of the higher value of the RA job is that of working with residents and making things better. Filling out paperwork is just not important to them.

ENFPs need personal interest and contact in their learning environments. They need to have a personal connection with presenters and feel that the presenter has an interest in them and their development. While they enjoy working with others in groups, they often find that the group is not effective in actually doing any of the work required. Training sessions should allow them some freedom and independence, even if it is just the ability to ask questions and raise issues and ideas for the group.

The imagination of the ENFP has to be used so that the material is fully taken in and made real. Being able to make projections about how the information can be used whether group projects, role-playing, or other activities, is very important to them. Their focus on possibilities means that they enjoy thinking about how the information can be used. Designing opportunities for them to brainstorm about the thoughts and concepts raised during training allow them to gain the most from the material.

ENFPs like to be exposed to a broad range of materials and topics and they enjoy finding relationships and patterns in the material. Able to handle complex and sometimes abstract material, the ENFP can understand many of the why's of residence life. This understanding can go a long way in improving their attitude and appreciation of the administrative and other bothersome parts of the job. For them, presenting the reasons for action before telling them how to act is the best plan.

Work Environment

ENFPs are fun-loving individuals who value their independence and ability to be creative. They want a place where people contribute and there is a team approach to doing things. ENFP RAs want to be a part of everything and they want to share in the responsibility for making things happen. This translates into a need for their work to mirror these values. Having flexibility and freedom in the performance of their job is as important as enjoying it. Their environment needs to be colorful and pleasant both in appearance and atmosphere. Work should be fun!

For the ENFP, work also needs to be meaningful. They want to have an impact on the larger world around them and to feel that they are making a difference somehow. Because they need to see that their efforts are having an effect, the RA job will be very attractive to them. Being able to directly act and improve the life of their residents gives a great deal of meaning to their activities, and the job will be more than a just pay-check for them. Their interest in the potential of others is an optimistic view that seeks to bring out the best in those around them. ENFPs are the staff cheerleaders.

The ENFP loves to brainstorm. Coming up with ideas, creating new ways of doing things, and starting new projects are areas in which they thrive. Their difficulty lies in staying with a project long enough to finish. Initiating new programs is their strength, but they prefer to rely on others to see those programs through to their completion.

The ENFP is the essential people-person who truly needs for everyone to get along. When conflict and disruption exists among their group, residents, or fellow staff, they direct all their attention and energy towards fixing the problem. Relationships always take precedence over tasks and the ENFP will want the group to deal with the conflicts before trying to do the job. This can cause problems when others, especially the ones in the conflict, do not feel the same way.

The ENFP Leader

ENFP RAs are charismatic, dynamic, and natural leaders who often jump to the forefront of any group they are in. Their enthusiasm for working with others, especially if it is a new project or event, makes them the natural choice when looking for someone who can motivate and engage others. This ability often allows them to get others excited about new ideas and plans, and often leads to the success of projects by just their friendly and energetic approach to the group.

ENFPs are quick to take charge of a group, especially if one of their cherished values or ideals are involved. Issues and concerns that affect people are especially important, and they quickly take ownership and fight for those issues with great energy and enthusiasm. They have a strong sense about making others happy and successful, and their causes are those that promote those ideals.

The ENFP leader is someone who is very aware of others in the group. Paying great attention to the needs of their group, they provide encouragement and opportunity for others and are quick to show appreciation for their work. The ENFP is able to provide the motivation for growth, change, and development in the group. Their awareness of the needs of their group allows them to provide the necessary motivation and recognition to help everyone function better. Using their energy and enthusiasm, the ENFP is able to get the group moving and keep it going.

Programming

With their flexible and fun-loving nature, the ENFP usually makes a good programmer once they deal with some personal issues. Their natural tendency to think and come up with ideas allows them to develop some really creative and interesting activities. The problem comes when they actually have to settle on one program. Their love of possibilities can sometimes paralyze them and prevent any program, however well thought out, from ever becoming a reality. When they are finally able to see their plans through, they can usually produce some very good programs.

Their spontaneous nature also means enables them to come up with fun activities and programs to develop the communities on their floor. Coming up with games, discussion groups, or stress relievers on the spur of the moment is very natural for them and, they are able to make the program work. This freedom is very important to the ENFP and should be encouraged whenever possible when they have this freedom.

ENFPs also tend towards programs that are designed to build confidence in their residents. Activities that show support and encouragement for their residents allow them to show their interest and concern for the success of their residents. Supervisors should help them design programs that promote the potential of their residents and help develop confidence, success, and involvement to help the residents succeed.

Organization

ENFPs are not organized, regardless of what they may think. They have a good ability to find what they need in the mess because they have created connections between people and information; this is how they can remember what is in a particular pile or place. No other person can use this system and it will be difficult for others if they have to rely upon the ENFP for guidance.

ENFPs are open to change and live in the moment. While they can adapt very well to emergencies, they also have a very flexible notion of time. Their value on personal needs can mean that they will be late and even miss obligations altogether if someone needs them. They realize that they are inconveniencing others and are often upset that they have caused problems, but in their prioritization of their world, people always come before meetings or other unimportant duties.

The ENFP is usually very interested in being better at managing time and space and will pursue learning about how to make improvements. They read and research ways to be more punctual, more organized, and more efficient. They find methods and plans and ways to be better focused on what's important. But they just do not use what they learned. Despite a genuine desire to be more organized, they just do not value it as highly as their need to be free, flexible, and open.

Lastly, the ENFP often has a very difficult time in planning how much time is needed for any particular activity or project. Because they are able to come up with ideas rather easily and quickly, they believe that making the idea a reality will be just a fast. This often results in them running late or out of time completely and being forced to try and rush to finish their work. ENFPs should learn how to be more realistic about what is involved in their projects and plan accordingly.

Relationship with Residents

ENFP RAs usually have a very good rapport with their residents as their social nature and appreciation of others give them many of the tools RAs need to succeed. Their ability to connect with others and appreciate individual gifts and abilities allows them to value each member of their floor for his or her own unique personality. They also have a strong sense that people are the ultimate concern and are willing to put other things aside whenever someone is in need. While this can cause problems in some situations, it does tend to establish a reputation as being helpful and available when their residents need them.

ENFP RAs are also very good at getting their residents involved, especially in activities and projects that they are interested in or working on already. Their enthusiasm for everything enables them to develop their community well as residents join in the excitement. When the ENFP is involved in other activities outside of housing, they try to get their residents involved in those as well. Whether working on special projects such as community service, involvement in Greek letter organizations, or other campus activities, the ENFP is a great ambassador for getting involved in the campus community.

Issues of Concern

Among the issues that ENFPs have to deal with is their ability to get swept up in all the possibilities and potential around them. Filled with ideas, they can often become paralyzed by the options and are unable to make a decision simply because they cannot decide what they like best. This often results in them making decisions and then making sudden changes. Overnight decisions about major, career choice, even the RA job, are not uncommon and, although they may not be ill considered, are the result of the conflicts that the ENFP is trying to resolve.

Part of this problem lies in the fact that the ENFP has a difficult time saying no to projects or activities, especially ones that are interesting. They have difficulty looking at their commitments in a realistic manner and setting priorities for what they want to accomplish. The ENFP wants to do it all and often tries to do just that. Burn-out or overload is very common for this type as the result of an honest desire to do it all, and not a lack of understanding of the work involved.

ENFPs also have difficulty knowing when it's time to think and when it's time to act. They enjoy brainstorming so much that they often do not feel the need to actually do something with their thoughts and plans. They want to continually come up with ideas and ways to do things. Actually doing something is just not as intriguing as figuring out all the different ways it can be done. This can mean that they often do not complete the work because they do not use their time to the best advantage.

Planning out appropriate time and energy for each phase of an activity is not in their nature. They go into things full speed and then will often run out of gas before getting across the finish line. This is a source of major conflict with others as the ENFP is not really bothered by not finishing a task. They would much prefer to just start it and for someone else to finish the job.

ENFPs can also be trying to a supervisor, as they often push at the boundaries and rules to see just how far they can go. This testing is not meant to be malicious or destructive, but rather it is an effort to exert their own independence and see how much they can shake things up. As residents and staff members this can get the ENFP in trouble, especially if their supervisor is a conformist and does not have the sense of adventure that defines the ENFP.

The ENFJ Resident Assistant: The Humanistic RA

The ENFJ RA is a social and lively individual who quickly makes friends and establishes good relationships. Their enthusiastic nature makes them quick favorites of others and enables them to quickly build community and connections among their residents and fellow staff members. They possess a warm and likeable personality that directs them into activities that promote the welfare and development of others. ENFJs prefer to make things better for others and the RA job is very suited to their temperament.

ENFJs are very aware of the people they work with and they quickly discover the hopes and dreams of their fellows. They work diligently to help others reach those goals and use their vision and organizational strength to help people create a plan to make those goals a reality. The ENFJ truly appreciates other people, not just for what they do, but also more importantly for whom they are. This appreciation is usually noticed and welcomed by those who the ENFJ favors.

ENFJs like the social aspects of their job. They enjoy working and interacting with others and seek to involve people in what they are doing. By defining their job as creating and maintaining the community, ENFJs work tirelessly to make it happen. But they do not do it alone. ENFJs strive to get everyone to take a role in making the environment a good one and seek to make everyone happy. This can cause them problems when conflict arises.

Personal values are critically important to the ENFJ RA. They need to feel that their work is meaningful and that their personal values are reflected in the responsibilities, policies, and activities of their job. They seek out jobs that allow them to express these values and work with people who share their feelings. The needs and growth of people is the central theme of their efforts and when policies do not reflect that value, they can have a very difficult time.

Training

ENFJs learn best in situations that are structured, but allow for individual creativity and personal expression. Having a guide to what they are doing is necessary for them to progress, but they do not enjoy having the opportunity to input their own individual thoughts and ideas. By allowing them, and others, to share their thoughts and ideas about the material, the ENFJ can be actively engaged in the learning process.

As a general rule, ENFJs make great students due mostly to their desire to please others, namely the presenter. They also enjoy it when the material is about something that appeals to them, namely people. Material presented about student development, counseling, and other helping subjects will be not only appreciated by the ENFJ, but also devoured. The trick is to get them to view the other less obviously people-related material (i.e., administrative tasks) in the same light. Explaining how others use the material, how it is used to help residents, and the values (non-economic) of the tasks help the ENFJ focus. Their organizational skills are usually good enough so that once the skill is understood, they perform it well.

ENFJs enjoy learning ways to socialize and have positive relationships. Learning about people and how to get along with them is very valuable and they spend enormous amounts of energy to master those subjects. Training on ways to communicate and understand their residents are very important to them and they enjoy those experiences.

Finally, ENFJ RAs are social learners. They need to work with others to achieve their best results. They prefer thinking aloud so that the group can come up with the best results. They also use their influence to make sure that the results show the attention and concern that they have for other people's needs. ENFJs are often the spokesperson for any group due to their personal charisma and ability to speak.

Work Environment

ENFJs want to work for an organization or group that is dedicated to making things better for others. The RA role, if marketed in the right way, is seen as a great opportunity for the ENFJ to not only help others personally, but to improve the efforts of the department. They are people-oriented and usually end up in a career that serves the needs of others, and the RA job allows them to begin that work early.

ENFJs needs an environment that provides them with a structure as to what is expected of them, but one that also allows them to make their own impression on the position. Creativity and freedom are highly valued and the ability to bring their thoughts and experiences to the position develops their allegiance and loyalty. Loyalty is very important to them as so much of their personal energy is based upon their relationships with others. They need to be able to not only give that loyalty to their organization, but to feel it from their leaders as well.

ENFJs enjoy work that, while structured, is not boring. They enjoy having a sense of what is going to happen, but not necessarily the same thing every day. The RA job allows them to plan for activities, projects, and tasks within a framework of unplanned possibilities. Their ability to be flexible and respond to sudden needs, especially those of the residents, allows them to stay enthusiastic about their work without worrying about sudden changes. This attitude of unplanned events in a planned structure allows the ENFJ to combine the best elements of being able to respond to residents' needs while remaining organized to their personal and job-related responsibilities.

The ENFJ Leader

The ENFJ leader is a highly enthusiastic person who motivates others through his/her own personal level of motivation for the project or the job. They will sell the organization if they believe in its values and benefits. Their sense of loyalty to the group makes them a very strong advocate and this often allows them to attract others to the group that they are committed to.

ENFJs enjoy leading groups, especially when there is something to be accomplished. Leading projects or committees allows the ENFJ to spend time on developing the relationships among the group members while also making sure that the tasks are accomplished. They respond well and quickly to the needs of their group and will actively engage others in making decisions about projects and organizational goals.

Conflict is an area that the ENFJ will struggle with and try to avoid. In their desire to make sure that everyone is happy, they often avoid discussions or issues that may lead to disagreements or arguments. ENFJs should learn to see the educational value in conflict and how conflict can be managed to produce good results. Once they see how dealing with conflict can help others, they will then be more willing to confront it. Training should allow them to discover how unresolved conflicts can cause the community to fall apart and cause the problems with and among residents.

Programming

The ENFJ RA is a fun programmer who sees programs as ways to bring residents together, get everyone involved, and be creative. Loose guidelines as to what is required will be best for ENFJs as it allows their independent creativity to shine.

With their organizational skills, ENFJs are good at planning programs and carrying out the tasks to make them happen. They usually do well with the necessary administrative tasks, but they need to see these tasks in a human light to have value. Spontaneous programming is not their strong point, but they are usually flexible and can handle sudden opportunities.

Assessment is an opportunity for the RA to find out what the residents want and need in programming, and this is an area that the ENFJ RA loves. Their desire to involve the residents in the planning means that they want to know what the residents are thinking. Moreover, they want their residents to be thinking about programming. ENFJs can be very inspirational and their enthusiasm often results in a community of residents that are much more involved and connected not only with their RA, but also with what the RA is doing for them.

Organization

ENFJs are very organized people who see the need to finish tasks and projects. Their organizational system is based on the needs of the people around them rather than on themselves. ENFJs are very aware of their responsibilities and will accomplish them because of their desire to please others, especially those whom they admire or trust such as their supervisor.

Time is something that ENFJs are aware of. Whether it is a deadline or just a meeting, they seek to keep the people around them happy by meeting their obligations.

They struggle however when a deadline is looming and someone comes to them with a problem. If it has happened enough, they learn to finish projects with enough time for emergencies. If not, their being late is unusual and probably the result of an understandable emergency.

ENFJs are planners. They see the future and plan how they are going to get there. Setting goals and objectives comes naturally as does making sure that their goals are accomplished. Their focus may be on keeping their relationships with everyone in a healthy manner, but they stick to their plan whenever possible. Being able to provide for the needs of the people around them is critical and they use their organizational skills to make sure that they are able to provide this service.

Relationship with Residents

ENFJ RAs develop good ties with their residents. Their ability to see below the surface allows them to address the needs and desires of their residents and help them achieve those goals. Developing a person and getting him/her to be a better person is a driving force that motivates the ENFJ. They see the RA job as a way to make that happen, especially if they also had an RA who had a powerful influence on them.

Counseling is an area in which ENFJs excel. Their interest in others, combined with an analytical ability to see issues and concerns, allows them to be a good sounding board and a source of support in times of trouble. Training that gives them the tools to help others is greatly appreciated, and they will use that training for their residents. Seeking out those in need, ENFJs are tireless champions of helping out others, sometimes to their own personal detriment.

While they have difficulty confronting conflicts, they can learn to see the value of what happens when unresolved situations lead to larger problems. They are usually able to deal better with issues that disrupt the community (e.g., noise) than those that only involve a single person or those that they feel is fair or right. Having to confront someone about something that they do not agree with is something that they have to work very hard at.

Issues of Concern

To the ENFJ, most things are very personal. This helps them deal with others as it allows them to create a personal connection and establish a good relationship. However, it can also be a problem. ENFJs can often get hurt or offended, often disproportionately, by the comments or thoughts of others. Criticism of the work they do becomes personal criticism of the ENFJ. This internalizing causes them to spin out of control and lose all sense of perspective. They take the criticism of a single aspect of their work and then begin to take apart all other aspects, even if those aspects are satisfactory or even appreciated.

They can also lose perspective in their relationships with the people and organizations that they develop connections with. Loyalty to people and groups is good, but it can often blind the ENFJ to the reality of a situation. They refuse to see problems or faults and even refuse to believe they exist. This causes them a great deal of difficulty when the person or group inevitably doesn't measure up in some situation. This sense of betrayal causes them to lose respect and allegiance for those involved, as well as lose their own motivation and enthusiasm.

Being aware that anyone, even someone they admire and respect, has limits and problems will help them to be more realistic in what they do and how they relate to others. Part of the difficulty is that often they are not very clear on what their own expectations are. Because they are so good at determining what others want and need, they expect that people can do it with them. Not recognizing their skill, they are often discouraged when others are not as intuitive as they are.

ENFJs also struggle with making people happy. Trying to do too much for others while not taking care of themselves can lead to exhaustion and burn-out. They also struggle with trying to be all things to other people. They also try to live up to what others think they should be, rather than finding out whom they want to be. Letting the people around them define them, they just wear out trying to meet those definitions.

ENFJs also struggle with their concern for harmony. Though they are able to recognize when the group is disruptive and work toward improving the group's relationships, they can sometimes lose sight of the group's overall goal. They will often put concerns about the tasks of the group after the personal issue, even if it means that the job is not done.

Finally, ENFJs should learn how to handle conflicts and other disruptive issues. They need to see how confronting concerns benefits their personal development, as well as others. From the person or persons causing the conflict to those who are adversely affected by it, everyone can learn from conflict, and in many situations is a necessary component for healthy growth and development. ENFJs need to understand that their initial impulse to sweep everything under the rug often results in more harm than good.

The INTJ Resident Assistant:
The Designing RA

The INTJ RA is an individualistic and very independent RA who is always looking for new methods and ways of doing things. They focus on what tasks or systems are in place and then work to improve those processes. INTJs believe that there is always another way of doing things and, if given a chance, will redesign their tasks and responsibilities in order to find that better way.

INTJs are intelligent and mentally deft in their learning and working with people. Generating new ideas and thoughts are very important to them as it is something that they are not only good at, but also greatly motivates them. Being able to set up new rules and procedures which they believe is better, allows them to bring out their own thoughts and beliefs. Anything can be improved.

Education is very important and they prefer the world of thoughts and ideas. Learning new things, constructing new ways of doing things, and planning for the future are all activities that engage their mind and attention. They find discovery to be one of the most interesting parts of their life and they constantly seek new things to find and learn about.

The INTJ is a very reserved person for whom socialization is neither a priority nor truly a need. As a result, they often tend to keep things inside and do not easily share their thoughts or feelings. Their independence is very strong and they do not rely on the approval or appreciation of others. Doing the job right is reward enough for them — praise and recognition from others is not their motivation — but they do appreciate when others recognize their skills and abilities.

When something is important to them they devote massive amounts of time, energy, and effort to making it happen. They work endlessly to make their ideas happen, even when those ideas may no longer be viable. They can be stubborn and headstrong and can refuse to let go of valued ideas even when the circumstances that gave rise to the issues have changed, and the plan or idea that they have created to solve those issues in no longer the best.

Training

INTJs love to learn. They are avid students and pursue subjects that interest them beyond any expectations of a teacher. The prefer to be challenged in their learning and want to find out the meaning and reasons behind why things happen, why things are done a certain way, and what it means for the future. There is rarely a point where the INTJ says enough.

Presenters, however, need to be prepared for the INTJ. They are quick to challenge authority about the views and information presented and if allowed, try to direct the training to reflect their own held beliefs. The best way to deal with this is for presenters to get the INTJ to where the presenter wants them to go. Rather than presenting conclusions, present the information and facts that will lead INTJs to the conclusion the presenter wants.

Routine and rote learning quickly turn off the INTJ. They need to be stimulated and will not absorb what is presented to them by a speaker or in a book. They prefer to have the opportunity to consider and evaluate the material in a personal way. In quick presentations they may not be very active because they are thinking about the information. Only after they have had a chance to digest and consider it will they share their thoughts.

Facts are not the most interesting things to INTJs. They want to know the underlying theories and beliefs about the world. They respond well to student development theories, ways to communicate, and patterns of how students grow and develop over time. Topics on specific details, such as administrative issues and forms, do not usually interest them.

INTJs will hold presenters to very high standards and expect them to know their material. If a presenter does not have material or sources to back up what is being presented, the INTJ is comfortable challenging their presentation or will simply disregard much of what is being said. Simply saying that something is a certain way without having information to support those claims results in the INTJ losing confidence and respect for the presenter.

Work Environment

The INTJ is an independent and strong-willed worker who prefers to operate with others of a like mind. They are quiet and reserved and slow to share their thoughts. The ability to operate in their own manner is very important to them. Privacy is very important to the INTJ and they need their own space or territory to function well. Teamwork is not necessarily the best idea for them personally. They want to be able to reflect and consider what they are dealing with before deciding how they want to continue.

INTJs have difficulty dealing with bureaucratic policies. They struggle with strict guidelines and procedures if they do not have the opportunity to make improvements to the suggested plans. It works best to help them see the critical components of any task (e.g., doing rounds) and then allow them the freedom to personalize or improve the suggested course.

INTJs are slow to share their thoughts unless those thoughts are about change. Getting into a process where they can discuss and plan change will energize and generate a great deal of enthusiasm from them. They enjoy looking at how everything interacts so that they can improve systems. This is good when you are reviewing for change; it can cause problems when change is not desired or necessary.

Competence is very important to the INTJ and they expect it from others. With their focus on tasks, this can result in conflicts when they work with others who may have different priorities. Nothing really excuses not doing assigned work, except extreme circumstances, and those exemptions are only granted grudgingly. Taking on projects is something they enjoy, especially when they can show a finished result. When others make this difficult or do not meet the expectations of the INTJ, trouble results.

INTJs are very future-oriented and are good at turning ideas into plans. Though not the best at brainstorming, due to the social interactions and its spontaneous nature, they are good at taking the goals and finding out how to get there. Their ability to see the organization as what it can ultimately become and do makes them strident advocates for improvement.

Because of their ability to see patterns and the underlying meaning behind what they do, INTJs are good at seeing possible consequences. They usually figure out meanings and potential results from the procedures and policies they encounter. Playing devil's advocate allows them to highlight weaknesses in the system; even if it's a relatively minor concern, it gives them the chance to exercise their strengths.

The INTJ Leader

The INTJ is a tough leader. They have high expectations and plans and they want everyone, including themselves, to live up to those goals. They struggle with making sure that others are aware of those expectations. Involving others in the execution of plans is often a step that INTJs can forget, even if they remembered to get everyone together to determine the group's goals.

INTJs view leadership as being responsible for planning how the group will achieve their goals. They do not feel the need to do the job of others and are usually very good at giving others the independence to do those jobs. INTJs can however fail to recognize when other people need closer supervision or support. If they were in that position they would not want that close contact or control, and they assume that this holds true for others.

INTJ leaders enjoy being able to restructure group or organization. Being able to try new ways of doing things, and who does what, is something they enjoy. This is great when difficulties arise and the group needs to re-evaluate its purpose and roles. The problem comes in when the INTJ wants change simply for change's sake and not to address any real need.

INTJs need to learn how to show appreciation for others. Motivation is not a dirty word, despite what they may think. For an INTJ, just doing a good job is usually enough. They know whether they did good or not and they do not depend on someone else to tell them that. They have trouble realizing that other people do not always feel the same and need to be appreciated and thanked, even if it is just for doing the job that they were expected to do.

Programming

INTJs need some direction and assistance to make sure that they are providing the best programs. Helping them develop ideas for assessment allows them to find programs that the residents will not only enjoy but will participate in. Otherwise, they can spend a great deal of time and effort on programs that they feel are best for the residents, but which may not have any bearing to the reality of the residents' interests.

They do well in planning and producing programs that attend to their personal interests, but are not as comfortable with the more social or unimportant programs, which to them means anything that does not advance their learning. The INTJ however handles the administrative responsibilities associated with programming rather well.

Organization

INTJs are dedicated organizers who will constantly look for the best way to put everything where it is supposed to be. Rarely will they be satisfied with the current methods and will look for something better. It is not uncommon for them to keep re-inventing how they organize their thoughts and lives in search of the best way. Even when they find something they like, it will usually not last very long.

Part of their view of being competent means that they are seen as being skilled and doing what they are supposed to be doing. This encourages not only their organization but also their time management. Producing results is very important to them and they usually have a good system to make that happen.

As a result of their nature, INTJs can miss some important details when planning and organizing things. They are the quintessential big-picture people and, as such, they may miss some critical points or concerns because they dismiss them as irrelevant. This is often the human part of the equation. Feelings and relationships are not given much weight in trying to find the best solution, and they can be viewed as being insensitive to those affected by their methods.

Relationship with Residents

INTJs do not have the easy relationship with their residents that the extroverted types often have. Their reserved and private nature causes others to view them as distant and hard to know. They view their job as one of performing tasks and projects and usually struggles with developing personal relationships. When they do establish those ties, they are most likely to do so in one-on-one situations and not in big group settings. INTJs need support and extra assistance in preparing to act in those situations, such as floor meetings, to make sure that they are providing time and energy for developing the community's relationships, and are not being too task-oriented.

INTJs can be very tough when expectations are not met, both for themselves and for others. They can be viewed as unyielding and harsh in how they enforce rules because they rarely allow for special circumstances or exceptions. Helping them learn how to hold their residents to standards without unnecessarily intensifying those situations is very important.

Issues of Concern

INTJs are not very social personalities. Their reserved nature often gets them into trouble because others feel that they are either being uncaring or unapproachable. The truth is that they work best when alone and quiet, and they think that everyone else does too. They do not share their feelings or thoughts easily, except in very limited circumstances. They need to learn how to express what they are feeling and thinking and to be aware of how they are perceived by others, especially residents and fellow RAs.

INTJs focus on the tasks and duties for which they are responsible. This often means that they can forget the importance of maintaining good relationships in the group and this causes problems for those types that need that kind of attention. Their supervisors should explain to them how groups work best when the people involved get along and are happy. A good example for the INTJ is to compare the relationship activities to the grease in an engine. It keeps the parts working smoothly while eliminating friction.

The INTJ is someone with a vision. Sometimes that vision does not have much connection to the real world. INTJs can get an idea in their head and refuse to let it go even when the facts show that the idea may not be feasible. They will pursue that idea with great determination and try to make it happen. INTJs need to learn to re-examine their plans and to be open to the thoughts of others. People often have ideas and information that the INTJ may not have considered or felt was important that could be the deciding factor in the success of their projects.

INTJs are good at identifying problems and concerns in the goals and work in which they are involved. Others can often interpret this ability as criticism of the group's efforts. They need to learn how to present their concerns in a manner that considers the feelings of the people involved, as well as take time to recognize the good parts of the process. INTJs do not usually see the need to go over what is working, even if doing so would provide some needed motivation to the others involved.

Organization and planning are both activities that INTJs enjoy. They find pleasure in coming up with new ways of doing things and making sense out of the world around them. Unfortunately, they can sometimes get so involved in the planning and design work that they do not actually do the work the plan was intended to address. An INTJ can design the most elaborate filing system for the job, but never actually use it!

Supervisors need to help the INTJ recognize how others can interpret their actions and attitudes. It is not that they are wrong or right. The question is whether the message that they are sending is one that they want others to receive. Without being able to share their feelings and include others in what they are thinking and planning, INTJs can alienate the people around them while believing that everything is okay because the job is getting done. When this happens, the INTJ is caught off guard and may be unable to find a way to fix the damage without help.

The INTP Resident Assistant:
The Analyzing RA

INTP RAs are inquisitive and thoughtful. They always seek answers and want to know the reasons behind what they are doing and learning. While they may appear to be very quiet and reserved, they are carefully learning all that they can and processing that information. As long as the group is going where they feel the information justifies, they will remain quiet. However, if the group goes in the wrong direction, they will demonstrate how much they understand the issues and where the problems are within the proposed action.

INTPs want things to make sense. They look for the reasons behind what is going on and want to understand how things work and the rules of the game. INTPs however are not always interested in playing the game. While they enjoy learning how to do new things, they do not always apply that learning in their life. They may know how to change a tire, fix a computer, or organize an office, but they may choose not to ever apply those skills.

The INTP is a quiet and reflective thinker. They enjoy coming up with unique and highly-developed ideas for their life. Finding out the truth is very important to them and is a part of their lifetime quest. While they seek to find the rules, it doesn't always mean that they will follow them. For them it is not finding of truth or achieving the results that matters; rather the joy is in the search, exploration, and discovery.

INTPs are often underestimated because of their reserved nature. They are often perceived to be in agreement because they do not immediately state any objections. The truth is that they rarely want or need the input of others in their decision making. When they have reached a decision, which can be tough, they will then share their thoughts, often surprising those around them.

Change and pressure are not challenges to INTPs. Their flexible nature allows them to respond well to situations that can cause others to succumb to stress. They have a logical and future-oriented approach to situations, which often results in a structured view of how things should be done. They also have a very fluid approach to work which allows them to adapt to new situations very easily.

Training

INTP RAs love to learn. They enjoy the whole way in which they discover new information and ways of doing things. They are relentless in their search and analyze information with a professional's eye. INTPs are quick to find conflicts and weaknesses in the material they are working with. Presenters need to be aware and ready for the struggle because INTPs will push the presenter to not only provide the material, but to defend it as well.

INTPs understand theories quickly. They have the ability to see how the underlying basis of the information can or cannot work and they enjoy those topics that deal with the bigger picture. Developmental theories and other ideas that tell them how to plan for the future are of great interest to them. They are usually not very interested in the day-to-day details and they rarely put much effort into learning material that does not interest them.

INTPs can become very focused on a topic that really grabs their attention, and will spend extra time and energy in learning all that they can about it. They also ignore other areas of learning in favor of that one. INTPs often struggle to keep their focus on all of their studies, or on keeping up with a study. Their curious nature often leads them to change their direction quickly and move onto a new subject with little or no warning.

INTPs need quiet time to themselves to be successful at learning. While they may enjoy some aspects of working with others, they prefer to have privacy and quiet to truly master what they are learning. They are not very active or vocal participants in many group projects, especially if they are new or unsure of the others in the group. As they have time to process their thoughts and learn about the group's dynamics, they can become more involved. It takes a while for INTPs to get into a more active role, and they will be more likely to share their thoughts with others when these kinds of activities are held later in the training schedule.

Work Environment

The INTP provides vision and ideas for the group but are rarely interested in providing the work necessary to make their ideas reality. It is not that they do not believe in their ideas or that they are unwilling to put in the necessary effort; rather they are not really interested in producing a final product or result. For them, the enthusiasm is in imagining the possible, designing what can be. Actually producing the program, building the model, or implementing the new system is, for them, a big letdown from the creative process.

INTPs like to enjoy what they are doing and, when they do, they have an almost endless supply of energy. They can focus and spend enormous amounts of time and energy toward their vision and making it a reality. It may not be to actually create what their idea is, but rather to know what that vision truly is. For example, they may spend a great deal of time designing how to have the best community on their floor. They can plan for programs, social interactions, passive activities, etc. But they may not actually do what their plan calls for because it is the planning that they love.

The INTP is a very independent thinker who prefers to have quiet and privacy to work. This can cause problems in the RA job, as the INTP has to deal with all of the people in the hall. While they may enjoy the interactions on some level, they probably prefer to do their job with as little contact as possible. Once they are ready to interact, they will do so. INTPs prefer to work in highly-flexible and unstructured environments. Their nature causes them to want the most freedom possible to do their jobs and make things happen. INTPs hate meetings and usually try to avoid them whenever they can.

As part of their independence they want to be the ones deciding on their goals and objectives, and to a certain extent, their rewards. Their supervisors need to work with them to plan out what the RAs should accomplish, how goals will be measured, and what the results will be. Taking a more team-oriented approach to setting objectives means that they are not only more invested in those goals, but that they will be more willing to operate within the supervisor's guidelines. Getting the INTP to buy into the standard rules and procedures can be tough, but by giving them input and opportunity to present their insights, they will be more willing to adhere to those rules even if they do not totally like them.

The INTP Leader

As a leader, INTPs will focus on the vision and principles of the organization. They are more interested in the foundational concerns of the group, why it is there, what it is doing, etc, rather than what projects or activities they will complete. They use their analytical skills to find where the group is having difficulties and problems, and look for ways to solve those issues and make the organization more effective. INTPs also look at how their organization is taking care of all aspects of the group (members, projects, purpose, etc.) and try and improve all of those aspects.

INTPs do not usually end up in the traditional leadership roles because they prefer to work either behind the scenes or in positions that are unique and allow their independence. Taking on special projects that focus on more internal concerns, rather than projects to be completed, are more their style. They would love to take charge of the group that is reviewing the organization's goals, purpose, or other intangible issues. They usually leave the roles that are focused on the people or events to others.

INTPs should remember that they are the leader of their floor in all aspects, and not just the ones that they prefer. Taking responsibility for programs, building community, and connecting with their residents have to be continually reinforced to them, whether internally or by their supervisor. They also need to remember that just because they cherish their independence and want it in their actions and position, it does not mean that everyone else feels the same way. They need to remember that for some resident types, they will have to take a more active role in providing support, direction, and motivation to keep others on track.

Programming

INTPs are good at planning the kind of programs that they want to do. Using programming models and other theories that tell staff the kinds of programs a particular community will best respond to is something that the INTPs not only enjoy but will usually throw themselves into. With the proper supervision, they can find assessment to be a great tool in their goal of building their community; the difficulty is in getting them to see the final result. INTPs need to see their programs as steps along the way to a larger goal, that of building their community or developing their residents. When they see programs in this light, they are more likely to actually complete a program instead of just thinking about it.

While they may struggle with planning and carrying out programs from an organizational perspective, they are very good at responding to sudden opportunities. Being able to do spontaneous or unplanned programs allows them full reign of their independent and freedom-loving nature. While they need encouragement and support to finish the programs they need, they will have a better mental view of programming if they are able to do programs that are not so structured.

Handling the details and administrative concerns with programming, such as forms and finances, is not of great interest to INTPs and they probably do not handle those tasks as well as others. They tend to focus on other issues and they are more likely be right at the wire for producing programs that have a scheduled date or deadline. Seeing the programs as part of a larger system for their floor helps them plan programs for a whole semester. While they may not need to organize their efforts to a high degree, such as setting dates of programs for the whole semester, they can come close. Planning programs for time periods that allows them some independence and ability to adjust as other things develop is important for them. Supervisors can then help the INTP finalize details as those time periods approach.

Organization

Although INTPs are not organized, it does not mean that they do not know how to organize. At some point, they usually look into ways of being more efficient by finding or creating the perfect filing system, getting the date book or other planner to list all their responsibilities, and so on. The problem is that they rarely use it once they understand how to manage their time and commitments. Actually doing it is just not in their nature.

INTPs do organize their thoughts and their ideas well. In fact, the most of their efforts at organization are directed internally, and are not visible to others. They have a cluttered and chaotic personal and office space and a system of doing things that few people could hope to understand, but this is because they are concerned with bigger things. Organizational priorities are the drudgery that they prefer to avoid.

INTPs are also collectors. They keep things on the chance that they may need it again in the future. This, combined with their lack of organizational priority, often means that their space looks overwhelmed. While they are quite happy working in their own systems, those that have to share their space or depend on them for materials or information often have a great deal of stress trying to find some kind of compromise.

Relationship with Residents

INTPs are not social animals and usually have a very small circle of social acquaintances whom they consider are friends. It takes them some time to develop their relationships with their residents, and on their own terms. Spending time with their residents means that they will have to build their connections on a one-to-one basis, and they will probably struggle with those personalities that are different from their own. Helping them to see how they can establish connections as RAs without the deep personal commitment that are necessary for their personal life will help them be more effective on their floor.

INTPs also struggle with their image of distance and unapproachability. Their inward focus often gives the impression that they do not want to be disturbed or infringed upon. Others can misinterpret this as a warning to leave the INTP alone. They can become distracted by their own thoughts and do not even realize that they are sending out that signal. If they are approached, they may respond well or still appear distracted. One way of helping INTPs is by warning others about their distraction, which can ease potential difficulties for them.

Issues of Concern

Below are several things that INTPs have to be aware of to operate at their best, and which their supervisor needs to help them watch out for in their work and personal development. First, INTPs need to be more forthcoming with their thoughts. Because they internalize what they are thinking, they do not share their issues and concerns and often just state a conclusion without providing any reasons. Just saying something won't work is not enough of a contribution; they need to identify problems that they see so that the group can come up with answers that the INTPs could not find on their own.

INTPs focus on problems because that is what they see as needing attention. They do not spend time celebrating what is working or what is done well because they operate on the assumption that things should be done right and an expectation has been met. INTPs need to learn to spend an appropriate amount of time showing appreciation for things done well and towards the people that did them. Other types do not get the same sense of accomplishment from just doing a job and need recognition for their efforts. INTPs need to learn how other people are motivated and how they like to be appreciated.

INTPs should also learn how to express their concerns and issues with projects and procedures in more positive ways. Just complaining about things or wanting instant change will not always get the results that they are looking for. They need to learn how to handle their concerns with others in a non-threatening or judgmental way. By presenting their thoughts positively to others, the INTP is more likely to succeed in their efforts, which is the whole motivation behind their behavior.

This critical approach to things is not just external, but is also often turned inward. INTPs can be very self-critical about their performance, ability, and accomplishments. They need to have some perspective and input from others about what they are doing. They can easily see what they are not doing or doing poorly, but they have difficulty recognizing their achievements and strengths. This causes them to become disheartened with their job, much to the surprise of their supervisor who thought everything was going well. Because they are so independent and self-motivated, others can forget that the INTPs can also be too critical of their own efforts to the point that they lose motivation and interest in their work. Providing them with feedback and encouragement, even though it may seem unneeded, can keep the INTP in a positive mental state.

INTPs sometimes spend too much time on theories and ideas and do not pay enough attention to the practical matters. Details and specifics are areas that the INTP struggle with, but they need to pay attention to them. It is very easy for the INTP to get absorbed in the abstract and esoteric parts of their work that they lose sight of reality. Keeping their feet on the ground while they work is very important and their supervisors will need to remind them of that. The INTPs are big dreamers because they can see so much potential in the world around them. Because of their desire for more information they can spend all their time gathering information until there is no time left to actually do the job. Just because they can see issues and think of alternatives rather quickly does not mean that they can finish the job just as easily. The INTP needs to be more realistic about what efforts are required to actually do the job.

INTPs should also be more aware of their own feelings and emotions. They are too likely to keep those feelings bottled up until it gets to be too much and they explode. These outbursts are seen as very atypical for them, but until the INTP learns to express their feelings in a healthier manner, they will continue the cycle of suppression and explosion. They can become more adjusted and happier by finding social outlets and even physical activities that provide an alternative to their inwardly-focused lives. Taking time to do things that are not connected to their big thoughts allows them time to recharge and relax.

The ENTP Resident Assistant:
The Competitive RA

The ENTP is an outgoing person who enjoys looking for new and different things. They have a great ability to adapt to situations and enjoy working in environments where they can use their ability to respond to changing circumstances. ENTPs enjoy figuring out how to do things, especially from a broad perspective. They enjoy understanding systems, models, and theories about how things are supposed to operate, and especially enjoy creating or designing new systems. Their ability to improvise makes them very good at handling crisis.

ENTPs do not like routine or other dull activities. They prefer innovation and look at the tedious tasks that come with their job as difficulties that they must endure, and try to avoid them whenever possible. They prefer to be flexible and creative in what they are doing and standard operating procedures can drive them to distraction. Dealing with bureaucratic systems that do not personally make sense is very hard on them. With their keen insight and logical mind, they are quick to find the faults and errors in the procedures and when an authority cannot logically explain why something is done a particular way, they are likely to write off that authority. Making sense is very important to them and when they hear that the reason is "just because," they may obey the guidelines but without respect for the person or organization.

ENTPs are risk takers. They enjoy trying out new things and ways of performing their tasks to keep their interest level high. They also enjoy the challenge of doing something better than before. Their outgoing and friendly nature allows them to avoid ruffling the feathers of those they work with — they truly just want to have fun. They can be tough, however, when it comes to what they expect of themselves and others. They want others to show competence in their jobs, especially a peer or a supervisor. While they will work with people subordinate to them and try and help them improve, they have little patience for those who should know how to do better but do not.

A very independent person, the ENTP can often disregard the rules in his/her quest to get things done. While they are very good at coming up with new ideas and analyzing problems, they just do not do as well when it comes to following procedures set up for everyone. While they may recognize the value of it for others, they prefer to stay flexible and react to situations as they occur. ENTPs want to stay fresh and excited about their jobs and they do not see that happening if they are forced into ruts or other drudgery, which is how they often view the established ways of doing things. To help them work on this, supervisors should encourage them to make suggestions for changes for the whole system instead of just wanting personal exemptions.

Training

ENTPs love to learn new things. They do not particularly like facts and other details, but want to know the underlying reason behind what is happening. The ENTP wants to figure out the why's behind the decisions that are made and the results that occur. It is important for them to understand all this, and they especially enjoy talking and debating with others to sharpen their own understanding. While they may not actually demonstrate their knowledge in traditional academic settings (such as tests) they show it when competition occurs. Being able to debate or show off their knowledge gets the ENTP to show their understanding rather quickly.

For the best results, ENTPs prefer to be able to discuss what they are learning. Group activities are good, but the they prefer being able to argue and debate what should work and what the material means. ENTPs do very well in brainstorming and other planning activities where they can theorize and come up with solutions to problems and issues that they face as a staff member. The ENTP struggles when they are forced to work alone or when they are required to just fill-in-the-blanks. They need to exert their independence and freedom by coming up with their own way of doing things. Explaining why certain procedures are standard and why they are important (assuming the reasons are logical) helps them see the value and pay attention.

ENTPs like to be challenged in their education. They doggedly pursue those subjects that interest them, to the point of independently searching out resources and other avenues that provide them with information about that particular topic. Presenters would do well to indicate where additional material, as well as contrasting viewpoints, could be found. ENTPs love the dynamic that results from opposing views and while they prefer it in a real-life setting, reading opposing views is a good substitute. Dry facts and details never hold their interest, except when they show how a system or policy does or does not work. ENTPs want their facts and theories to all line up, and they are one of the quickest types to see when that does not happen.

Work Environment

ENTPs like to work where innovation and excitement are part of the daily life and the RA position can provide that. The biggest challenge is their inability to implement serious changes to how things are done. If their supervisor can channel their creative energies toward their residents, then they may see some positive results. The problem is that ENTPs, while being great idea generators and planners, are not really interested in seeing through the projects that they create. They would rather have someone else handle that aspect of the job.

ENTPs like their freedom and want the flexibility to do their work as inspiration and motivation hits them. Being able to improvise and respond off-the-cuff is one of their strengths, and the ENTP relies on it rather than on careful planning or preparation. While they may work well in those situations, they run into difficulties when their experience is not enough to give them the material they need to respond to sudden changes. For example, when getting ready for that first floor meeting, the ENTP RA in their second year wings it much more successfully than their first-year counterpart, even though both may approach the meeting with a rather loose plan for the event.

A great asset to an organization, the ENTP has a very positive outlook, especially when it comes to dealing with problems. They see difficulties as challenges to their abilities, and being able to overcome those challenges provides them with a great deal of self-motivation. This enthusiasm for challenge is often contagious and can help their group approach difficulties with a much more positive attitude. They like to take risks and appreciate it when others recognize their abilities and talents.

The ENTP Leader

ENTP leaders are very outgoing people who want to not only make a difference, but want to be seen doing it. They want to have a visible effect on the organization and the people around them, and like to be appreciated for their creativity and innovations. They enjoy designing models for how the organization can function and how they can perform their tasks, but they prefer to let others take the responsibility for actually seeing the plans through. ENTPs enjoy what they are doing and fun is an important part of keeping their motivation levels high.

For ENTPs to want to do something and to take responsibility or leadership, they need to see that what they are doing is meaningful. There needs to be a reason for what they do. Finding meaning in their work is very important and the organizations and groups that they take an interest in will usually share this goal.

ENTP are very independent and feel that having the freedom to do their work is very important. It is also something that they feel is very important with regard to others. ENTPs are good at helping others to be less dependent and better able to stand on their own. Although they enjoy the social aspects of group work and team activities, it is with an understanding that all of those involved share their level of competence. It is more a case of a group of stars all working together than a team with one or two stars and a crew of supporters. They want everyone to be as good as they are because that is when the best results happen.

As leaders, ENTPs can sometimes be unrealistic about the capabilities of the people they work with. While they want to promote independence, they do not always provide the support that others need to succeed. For them it is often a case of letting others do or die and it is up to the ENTPs to make it work. By giving them the freedom to do the job, they expect it done. By not providing the initial support or continuing encouragement that some types need, ENTP leaders can often lose their followers.

Programming

ENTPs are good at planning programs and finding out what their residents like. Being social persons, they can quickly figure out what is going to work for their residents. They will find their own programming model to use if they feel that the department's model is not effective. In working with a special population, the ENTP is very good at figuring out what is going to succeed. The supervisor can help direct this effort by working with the ENTP RA in defining what a successful program is and what it is meant to accomplish. By leaving it up to the ENTP, criteria may be weighed very differently from the department's and can result in the ENTP having a very strong opinion about their way of programming.

Their organizational skills usually mean that handling the administrative tasks of programming will not take the highest priority. Turning in paperwork and following the procedures will be an effort for them, but by using their competitive nature a supervisor can improve their response. ENTPs are usually good at impulse programming where their independence and sense of freedom allow them to respond to a situation without consulting or asking for permission. Setting up some pre-approved programs that the ENTP can present whenever they feel the need, or allowing them some flexibility in the approval process, help keep their motivation level up.

Organization

ENTPs, like most of the perceiving types, are not really good organizers. While they do have a system, and it is one that usually works well only for them, and is not understood or managed by anyone else. It is the energy and passion for creating ideas and plans that drives them, not the mundane tasks of actually making those plans a reality. This separation causes them to misjudge the amount of work involved and what they can reasonably give to those projects. They often over-commit themselves to projects and do not follow through on all of their obligations. It is not a lack of desire to do the work that hurts them; it is their lack of understanding of what is involved.

ENTPs focus on the big picture and often miss the details and facts of what they are doing. Lists and calendars do not hold their interest. While they may try to use such organizational tools, it is never natural and they slip back into old habits rather easily. Time management is also a problem for them. With their inaccurate understanding of how much time and effort are involved in any project or work, they are often running to appointments because they just did not prepare the time needed. Helping ENTPs to say no to opportunities and teaching them to be more realistic about what is involved will be of great help.

Relationship with Residents

ENTPs are social RAs who can relate to many people on a casual level. The are fun-loving and outgoing and like to enjoy what they do. If they have set their eyes on the RA job as being worthwhile, their enthusiasm for the position and the opportunities it gives them will usually show through. The ENTP RA is very good at motivating others on projects, specially on more abstract goals such as creating a positive community.

One area that can cause them difficulties with residents is their individual way of doing things. Because they are not always organized as others, conflicts can arise from their being late or forgetting some of the details of what they agree to do. While they do not consider this to be an issue, it can become serious if residents begin to see the RA as unreliable. This is something they do not want, and as their supervisor you can help them plan on how to avoid those kinds of situations.

The positive part of their personality is that the ENTP is usually up for sudden activities; their willingness to put things aside can make their residents feel very important and appreciated. While they may not take care of some of the basic concerns, they do pay serious attention to the big issues. ENTPs can become distracted by their grand ideas but they normally want to share their thoughts so others rarely feel the distance that their introverted counterparts project. While the ENTP may not have a thought-out agenda for what they are doing, they are usually fast enough on their feet that they still manage to look competent to their community.

Issues of Concern

ENTPs have to struggle keeping up with the reality of what is going on around them. While they are great at dealing with the future, the present is often lost and not given the attention it deserves. Details, facts, and specifics are all areas that they need to pay greater attention to. They also need to put some of the energy that they use in designing new systems to actually using those systems consistently so that all of their work do not go to waste. Finding the time to keep up with all aspects of their work is important, and ENTPs need to give honest consideration to how much of their time the work will require.

ENTPs also need to be conscious of their desire to win the race. When it comes to their work, especially the intellectual aspects of it, the ENTP can be very competitive and can fall into conflicts with the people that they are supposed to be working with. They have a very strong will and will often believe that their ideas are the right one to such a degree that they close out the possibility that someone else can offer something. This desire to be the one who finds the answer is useful in some settings, but it can result in a great deal of stress for those around them.

ENTPs love to do things and will often get involved in different activities to stimulate their minds and their energy. This often causes them to be over-committed and risk burning-out. ENTPs need to find social outlets to release their stress, learn to set priorities for their time and attention, and learn how to determine what a job or position will demand. Only when they are honest with themselves about how much work is involved will they be able to make plans for themselves that can succeed.

Because ENTPs can be one of the most assertive types, they need to be cautious of being too assertive. They have a strong desire to make a difference in what they do, but they can take it too far. By not taking the time to make sure that their ideas are well thought out, they can miss important things. When that happens, it can send them into a spiral. ENTPs want to be appreciated for their abilities and when something goes wrong they feel it looks bad on them, which is something they cannot stand. To look incompetent or unskilled hits them very hard and causes them to either withdraw or become even more competitive to prove their worth. Their supervisor needs to help them find a balance between their competitive and cooperative impulses, as well as provide them with impartial feedback so they can see themselves in a more honest light. Their supervisor also needs to pay special attention when things go wrong to help ENTPs find a better way of learning from the experience.

The ENTJ Resident Assistant:
The Executive RA

ENTJs are very forceful and take-charge people who have a natural skill at leadership and the ability to make others see them as not only an authority figure, but also as someone who knows what they are doing. They are quick to take care of problems and enjoy providing the necessary structure to the world around them. Organized and able to see future needs, ENTJs are adept at designing plans to help themselves, or the groups that they belong to, to both plan and accomplish their goals. ENTJs need to have goals and a plan; they do not enjoy uncertainty in their life and work hard to create a goal for themselves. ENTJs usually focus on the long-term and most of their decisions will be made with their plan in mind. For the ENTJ, nothing is supposed to happen by accident.

ENTJs are very strong willed people who rarely accept no for an answer, but rather they see it as a challenge. They see those obstacles as things that they are supposed to overcome and they are more than willing to rise to the occasion. For them, no simply means to try again, and try harder. ENTJs want control and power and they seek out those positions of leadership that enables them to have the control over things that are very important to them. ENTJs want to make an impact on the world and want others to see them doing it. Having the ability to decide on a course of action, for themselves and others, is very important to them.

Designing plans and strategies are very important to ENTJs and they are constantly working on them for themselves and their groups. They are able to come up with these strategies rather easily and they constantly look for ways to improve and find the best one for the situation. ENTJs can become very focused on this pursuit to the point of inadvertently closing out others or even causing them grief. ENTJs want to do the job the best way possible to complete the task and get the reward. If this ruffles feathers, so be it but the job will be done.

ENTJs are active people with a wide variety of interests and activities. They want their time and energy to be well-spent, so in order for them to get involved projects must make sense. Logical thinking and relevance are very important to them. For them to do a task or activity, they must be able relate it to the bigger picture and their overall plans and goals. They do not enjoy inactivity and are always planning what they will do next. You will not find them sitting still and waiting for things to happen; they are in the thick-of-things, usually leading the way.

Training

ENTJs enjoying learning, but it is always as a tool for their own advancement. Knowledge is valuable if it can be used in the future to make their goals and plans a reality. They want to be able to put their knowledge to use in their lives or their jobs, and they want to see a difference or a real result. Information is not just to know, but also to use. They like to experience a variety of methods from lecture to group activities, but they expect two very important things from those trying to train them. First, the presenter must be organized and provide the group with structure. There has to be a plan for what they are doing and not just some random experience. ENTJs are quick to identify when someone is winging it and that causes them to lose interest in the experience. Second, the presenter needs to demonstrate his or her own experience and ability with the material. Competency is very important for them to learn from someone and they need to know that the presenter actually knows what he/she is talking about.

ENTJs enjoys learning about how things operate and the systems that are involved. Figuring out the underlying meaning and methods to what they do is more important than the details or specifics. While they understand the need for those details and their organizational skills usually allow them to work with them fairly well, the truth is that those parts of training do not hold the interest that the big-picture studies do. Models, theories, and philosophies are all things that the ENTJ want to learn about and they also want the chance to discuss them. Arguing or debating about theories and meaning enables them to work things out internally, so group interactions help them out a great deal.

Work Environment

ENTJs enjoy working in a structured and organized setting with people committed to achieving the goals and objectives of the organization. It is the primary goal of the group to see results. The tasks that the group are supposed to be doing need to be done before any other considerations. Their job is very important to them and they so identify themselves by what they do that often they become the job, more so than any other type. This part of their highly competitive nature drives them to succeed and to take charge of their group.

As decision makers, ENTJs do not shrink from making hard choices and are willing to risk making people unhappy with their decisions. Taking a long-range approach, they will give up short-term gains or concerns if it means that they will win in the end. ENTJs want results and will take the steps necessary to achieve those results even if it makes other people unhappy in the process.

ENTJs are very good at dealing with problems facing a group or organization. They are organized and tough-minded and willing to take the lead in the group so that someone is making decisions. They are going to be interested in positions of authority and look for ways to continue their advancement and growth. Enjoying the complex nature of interactions and situations, the ENTJ is a master planner who knows what is going on with the organization and how to use the strengths of the people involved. If you want the job done, then an ENTJ is one of the best at making sure it happens.

The ENTJ Leader

ENTJs want to be leaders. They enjoy having control over themselves and to a certain extent over others. They often feel that they are the best person for the job and they pursue leadership opportunities that allow them to pursue their personal goals. The RA job is just a step on their path, but while they are on it they will usually give a great deal of their energy especially as it allows them to hold a very visible position of authority that has others see them as both important and responsible.

Because they are determined leaders, they often have difficulty following others unless they truly feel that person deserves their support. They need to see their leader not only as someone who is organized, capable, and deserving, but also as someone who is competent to do the job in their own right. If they find this person, ENTJs will seek to learn all that they can to gain whatever knowledge or skills they feel that person has. They are direct and hard to convince and are likely to challenge their leaders to make sure that they know what they are doing. If the responsibilities of the group are being met, then the ENTJ is happy. Completing the tasks is key whether they are the leader or not.

The ENTJ leader is one who will bring some long-range vision for the group. They will try and show the importance of having a plan for what they want to accomplish. If they cannot convince the others, they usually proceed with their plan anyway. ENTJs are good at making the people around them think. They can usually find ways to get others to come to the conclusion that they want without having to force or overwhelm others, although they can do that as well. By careful questioning, the ENTJ often gets others to the place the ENTJ wanted to go without the others even realizing it.

Programming

ENTJ RAs see programming as part of their job and are able to handle the administrative and other departmental expectations well. Their organizational skills allow them to keep up with what is involved in a program and they plan well for what they need to do. ENTJs are not spontaneous programmers as they prefer to work from their plan and not wing it. However if they are encouraged to be spontaneous, then they can at least appear that way.

ENTJs are outgoing people with a great deal of energy and enthusiasm that they can use to get others excited about what is going on. They are likely to want to work with others to make their programs larger and more successful, and will quickly plan out their programs for either the term or the whole year. While they may not share this information with their supervisor, it is probably being developed from the time that they know they have the job. Training ENTJs about programming models, and how residents have specific needs at certain times of the year and during their academic career, will provide them with ideas of what kinds of programs they should be doing.

ENTJs enjoy competition and strategic thinking and they can use these strengths to design some rather unique programs. They can come up with games and other ways to discover information in such a way that their residents not only learn but also enjoy the process. Since the ENTJ does not like to be idle, they must always be doing something and spending some of their time coming up with complex and thought-out activities for their programs. This can be a good challenge for them and their ability to think long range. Whatever programs the ENTJ ultimately decides to do will be part of their master plan for their community and will showcase the overall skill and ability.

Organization

ENTJ RAs are organized and they always have a plan and method in their lives. They are adept at using time-management techniques and probably have a rather developed organizer/planner or other system where they can keep up with their commitments. ENTJs are also aware of the time issues that surround them and expect that of others as well. If given the opportunity, ENTJs have no compunction about organizing things for the people around them as well as for themselves. They do not like disorder and, with their interest in systems and procedures, will, if given a chance, design entirely new ways of doing the jobs and tasks that are the responsibilities of their group.

Being able to make good judgments about what will take up their time and how much is involved in their work allows them to manage their commitments well. They do not have many issues with their ability to handle tasks and other responsibilities; their only issue is doing those tasks that they feel are not worth their time. However, they will still work at those because they do not want to appear incompetent or it affects their plans for future positions of authority and responsibility. ENTJs plan their course out and also likely have their job responsibilities set up to allow them to achieve all their expectations, and then some. They may not seem as flexible and free as the other types because they prefer to plan for contingencies and not be surprised. They will have thought about what they will do in certain situations that they may face as an RA and will probably be able to say what they would do in a particular situation, even if they never have to face it.

Relationship with Residents

With their outgoing personality, the ENTJ RAs will be at ease in front of a group and usually do well in creating connections with their residents. Because of their desire for respect and recognition of their abilities, they want their residents to view them as being good at their job and will put forth a great deal of effort to make this happen. While they may not be the easy going RA that some residents would prefer, they do have a good influence on their residents and their fellow staff members.

ENTJs are good leaders and quickly establish themselves as the voice of authority on the floor. They have a good grasp of what is going on with the residents, and are able to work with the residents while still doing their job responsibilities (duty, confrontation, etc.). With their outgoing nature and natural leadership skills, these RAs usually develop a good connection to their residents based on both respect and common connection. They are preparing to be the leaders of the world and they will demonstrate that ability within the hall.

Issues of Concern

ENTJs have to be aware that others can see their drive for success and control negatively. They may feel that because they know what is best others will agree, but this is often not the case. ENTJs need to work on being more inclusive of others and should take the time to give the people around them the ability to contribute and have an impact. Even if it does not change their original plan, giving others a chance to participate can help reduce unhappiness and increase support for their ideas. Being decisive is a strength of ENTJs, but they can take it too far. Making decisions faster than they need to, they can miss some of the details and pertinent facts that could lead them to a different result. ENTJs try to be seen as having leadership qualities and so they often make decisions without hesitation, even when hesitation is not a bad thing. They need to accept that they may not know everything, nor do others expect them to.

ENTJs are always thinking about the future and, while this works when they are planning ahead, it can hurt them in their day-to-day operations. While their organizational skills help them somewhat, they tend to ignore today in favor of tomorrow. They focus too much on what is going to happen that they forget to take care of what is currently going on, which gets them into trouble. It can also lead to problems when they do not take the practical realities of the world around them in their planning. By spending so much of their time and energy working on the future, they can cause more problems for themselves than their skills can handle when the consequences of those missed facts finally show up.

ENTJs are concerned about control, which is why they are good leaders. But sometimes they can get overworked and that concern becomes an obsession. When ENTJs get stressed out, then they can start seeing the input and comments of others as trying to take control from them. When this happens they are likely to blow up and strike out. While ENTJs are normally good about their emotions and thoughts, they do tend to bottle them up and when something sets them off it can be totally out of proportion to the actual triggering event. ENTJs need to be more sympathetic to the input of other people, even when that input is critical of their plans and ideas. By allowing those around them to feel comfortable enough to contribute or to challenge them, ENTJs have the best chance to succeed in their overall goals.

ENTJs need to give more energy to people and the relationships that exist between them. Sometimes they get so concerned about doing a job or a task that they will do whatever it takes to make it happen, even if the group responsible for the job ends up in ruin or destroyed in the process. They need to understand that some types need more attention and appreciation for not only the jobs that they do, but also just for who they are. ENTJs see so much value in doing their job that they forget that other people have different motivations. Supervising ENTJs will be a challenge for any type that is not similar to the ENTJ, but helping them realize the human factor in their work will be of great benefit to the RAs. Getting them to pay attention to the importance of relationships, sometimes even to the point of not doing the job, is a struggle but it allows them to become much more effective and successful leaders.

Chapter
5

Exercises and Applications

Exercises and Applications

The first warning about using type theory in supervision is that no system, regardless of how good it is, can apply to all people. Attempting to use this information to find the "best" RA type is strongly discouraged for a number of reasons. To start with, there is no "best" type for RAs, rather there are people whose natural tendencies will enable them to perform certain aspects of their job either easier or harder, but the final choice for how they will perform is ultimately theirs. It is a good idea to help your staff to better understand each other, to communicate more effectively, and to appreciate the differences that exist to help them be the best RA.

In the following exercises, the group is divided by preference pairs and given a situation or issue to resolve. By dividing the group along these lines, the goal is that the people in the group will come up with a consensus decision much more easily than they would if the other preference was mixed in with them. The value of this exercise is when each group reports its conclusions and the other group hears the approach they took.

Exercise 5.1 (T/F)

Facilitator: Divide the group of people into two teams, one made up of all the thinking (T) types and one of all the feeling (F) types. Tell each group to discuss the two versions of the problem and come up with a plan to deal with the problem. Each group will need to record their solution.

Susan and her roommate Rhonda are having an argument. As their RA, it is your job to help them resolve their problems. Both Susan and Rhonda have come to you separately to tell you about the issue and your supervisor wants to know what you are going to do about it. Read each story below and then, as a group, devise a plan for working with Susan and Rhonda, and then tell your supervisor about it.

Side 1 – Susan's Version

Susan tells you that there have been problems between her and Rhonda since the first day they moved in together. At the beginning of the year they filled out a roommate contract that specified the agreed rules about visitors and phone calls, but Susan says that Rhonda is constantly breaking it. She gets phone calls after the agreed upon cut-off time, she has guests over at all hours (not breaking visitation guidelines), and she is really messy.

Last week, Susan came home and found Rhonda and two friends. Susan left to go do some homework, hoping that the friends would be gone when she returned, but they were still there when she got back several hours later. They were talking loudly and were all over the room. Rhonda said that they were all helping one of the girls to get over a break up with her boyfriend and that the girl was very upset. Susan did not see anyone being upset, they were all laughing, being loud, and playing music. This is the last straw for Susan. Rhonda does not follow any of the rules and she wants to know what you're going to do about it.

Side 2 – Rhonda's Version

Rhonda does not understand why Susan is suddenly so upset. She says that they have had a few arguments over the term, usually about the phone and people stopping by to see Rhonda, but each time Rhonda has explained the unusual reasons behind the call or visit and Susan seemed to understand and said it was okay. She has apologized for the interruptions, but Susan gets upset even when she is not asleep. One time she got mad because Rhonda got a call late at night from her brother although Susan was up late watching a movie. It would be one thing if people were constantly calling and waking them up, but it seems that Susan wants absolute conformity, even if it doesn't disturb her.

The most recent problem has developed when one of Rhonda's friends, Emily, broke up with her boyfriend. Rhonda and some friends got together to cheer Emily up and ended up back in Rhonda and Susan's room. They got Emily to stop being depressed and were able to have fun and laugh and everything seemed to be going fine. Susan came in and after a few minutes left for the library. When she came back she got into a fight with Rhonda about her friends always being over. It was not past the time they agreed to have people over, nor was it very late in the day. Rhonda doesn't understand why Susan is always mad. She has tried to talk to Susan about what she wants, but all Susan says is that she is not following the rules. Rhonda asks you what to do.

Questions for the groups:

1) What are the key issues that Rhonda and Susan are facing?
2) Who is the most at fault in this situation?
3) What is Susan's problem with Rhonda?
4) What is Rhonda's problem with Susan?
5) What is Susan's role in this situation?
6) What is Rhonda's role in this situation?
7) What approach/plan do they have for resolving this problem?

Exercise 5.2 (E/I)

Facilitator: Divide the group into two parts, one with all of the extroverts (E) and one with all of the introverts (I). Each group will need to record their solution.

You have had the worst week of your life in college. It seems that everything that can go wrong has gone wrong. You have had troubles in class, on your floor, even in your personal life, and you are at the end of your rope. Your supervisor calls you in because he has noticed the stress you are under. He tells you that he expects you to take this weekend off and get some rest. What do you plan to do this weekend?

Questions for the groups:

1) What is the first thing you want to do?
2) What do you want to avoid this weekend?
3) How will you deal with your residents?
4) If you had some extra money to help you relax, what would you do with it?
5) What are some things you can do to keep from getting this stressed out again?

Exercise 5.3 (N/S)

Facilitator: Divide the group into two parts, one with all of the sensing (S) types and one with all of the intuitive (N) types. Each group will need to record their solution.

The assistant director has asked you to help select the new RAs for next year and wants you to come up with some ideas for making selection more effective and enjoyable for everyone involved. As you have gone through the process, you have some idea of what it was like and what you thought needed to be changed. As a group, come up with some suggestions for the assistant director.

Questions for the groups:

1) What is the goal of the selection process?
2) What attributes or abilities are you looking for in new RAs?
3) What are some characteristic traits of the candidates that would concern or worry you?
4) What steps in the process are not necessary and can be changed (if any)?
5) What steps in the process were the most valuable and useful?
6) Assuming that you will have an active role in the next selection process, what role(s) would you most like to take?

The next exercise focuses on combinations of preference types. In these exercises, the groups are divided using two of the preference pairs to respond to the scenario. Again, the major benefit from this exercise is through sharing the solutions that each group develops with the other groups.

Exercise 5.4 – Temperaments

Facilitator: For this exercise, separate the participants into four groups – NF, NT, SJ, and SP. Each group will need to record their solution.

This year your residence hall staff has enjoyed tremendous success in all aspects of your job. Your programs were well-done and achieved record numbers of participation from your residents. Judicial incidents were handled appropriately and all the administrative tasks were accomplished without any problems. During your staff meeting your supervisor tells you she wants the entire staff to attend the national RA conference in Orlando, Florida and to present a program on the new hall-wide program that you all created which has received a great deal of attention and praise.

You are all very excited and looking forward to attending. Your supervisor tells you that she will ask RAs from other halls to cover the building while you are gone. The next week your supervisor has bad news; it seems she forgot that the national RA conference is the same weekend when the Homecoming and Department of Housing policies require that each building have one-half of their RAs on duty all weekend. Because of this, there are no RAs available to cover your hall. Your supervisor got permission for one-half of the staff to go to the conference, but the rest have to stay and be on duty. She tells you that she wants you, as a group, to decide who gets to go.

Questions for the group:

1) How does your group react to this change?
2) What method are you going to use to decide who goes to the conference?
3) What are some issues that your staff needs to deal with in this situation?

Chapter

6

Closing Thoughts

Closing Thoughts

You now have the information you need to understand the 16 types of RAs according to the Myers-Briggs Type Indicator and Type Theory. That is not to say that you have all the information that you need for your staff, but you do have the building blocks. Working with any group of people, student staff or otherwise, means taking time to learn about each other and the personal quirks and differences that exist among them. With this work I hope to give you a solid source of information that can prepare you to work with your staff and help you identify the underlying source of problems when they arise. You, as their supervisor, will know how those problems will manifest in their job performance, and by using this work I hope that you will understand what their internal motivations and driving forces are.

This information is presented with a broad approach so it can be used with other residence-hall staff other than the traditional RA — undergraduate staff (peer advisors, computer assistants, desk staff, etc.), graduate staff, and even professional staff. With professional staff, how their personal type affects their supervisory style, as well as the recreation that they enjoy to ensure a good balance in their lives should be included. Additional material can also be presented to identify the teams that supervisors will be working with based on the group's individual types and how those types will interact with each other.

As a general guide, I feel that this work provides the reader with a good vision of what each RA type is going to be working with in their toolbox of personal skills. For example, if a supervisor is the executive type (ENTJ), he/she will have a better understanding of the needs and interests of *introverted, sensing, feeling,* and *perceiving* staff members.

Finally, it is important to remember that any type theory — or for that matter any theory of behavior, leadership, or management — should be used with caution and care. No system is exact or perfect and it is very easy to make sweeping assumptions based on the material contained in this and other books. For the record, I have found that the MBTI has amazing accuracy, and knowing the theory and meaning of the preference pairs has helped me in numerous occasions working with students in counseling, supervision, judicial, and everyday interactions.

This material is not designed, nor should it be used, to determine who would make the best RA based on their MBTI type. Just because someone has a natural tendency towards a certain behavior or attitude does not provide any guarantee about their performance. Neither does it mean that another person could not do as good a job. By reading the 16 types presented here, I hope you will see that each type has valuable skills and abilities to bring to any department and residence hall community depending on the person's willingness to work and the specialized needs of a floor (which is usually not known prior to the beginning of the school year).

I hope that the information found within will be useful and valuable in your work with residence hall staff and that it helps all those involved to see that there are many different ways to approach a position, like the resident assistant, and that each one of them has some validity. Although there may be staff members that are not living up to their ability, there are no bad types for the RA position. Their performance is a personal decision and is not a result of the type preference. Good luck in the halls and congratulations on taking the most important step in working with any person — having the desire to better understand another person.

Appendix

**Suggested Readings and
Additional Resources**

Suggested Readings

DiTiberio, J. K. and Hammer, A. L. (1993). *Introduction to type in college.* Palo Alto, CA: CPP Inc.

Hirsh, S. K., and Kummerow, J. M. (1990). *Introduction to type in organizations.* Palo Alto, CA: CPP Inc.

Hirsh, S. K., and Kummerow, J. M. (1989). *Life types.* New York: Time Warner Books.

Martin, Charles (1997). *Looking at type: The fundamentals.* Gainesville, FL: Center for Applications of Psychological Type, Inc.

Quenk, N. L. (1996). *In the grip: our hidden personality.* Palo Alto, CA: CPP Inc.

Additional Resources

Center for Applications of Psychological Type, Inc.
2815 Northwest 13th Street, Suite 401
Gainesville, FL 32609
www.capt.org
CPP Inc.
3803 E. Bayshore Road
Palo Alto, CA 94303
www.cpp-db.com